Messiah

THE COMPOSITION AND AFTERLIFE OF HANDEL'S MASTERPIECE

JONATHAN KEATES

BASIC BOOKS
New York

The sixty-four-year-old George Frideric Handel in 1749, corpulent and bewigged, in a portrait by Thomas Hudson that was owned by the composer himself.

CREDIT: PRIVATE COLLECTION / BRIDGEMAN IMAGES

Basic Books
Hachette Book Group
1290 Avenue of the Americas, New York, NY 10104
www.basicbooks.com
Printed in the United States of America
First published in 2016 by Head of Zeus, UK
First U.S. edition: October 2017
Published by Basic Books, an imprint of Perseus Books, LLC, a subsidiary of Hachette Book Group, Inc.

Print book interior design by Trish Wilkinson.

Library of Congress Control Number: 2017952758

ISBNs: 978-1-5416-9735-5 (hardcover), 978-1-5416-9749-2 (ebook)

LSC-C

10 9 8 7 6 5 4 3 2 1

CONTENTS

INTRODUCTION

The making of Handel's *Messiah* was an act of faith, in more senses than one, on the part of two remarkable men: the composer George Frideric Handel and his friend, the littérateur and musical enthusiast Charles Jennens. As devised by them both, the work represented an entirely new concept in the genre of sacred oratorio as understood during the mid-eighteenth century, hence there was no guarantee of a favourable reception at its earliest performances. In a cultural milieu so preoccupied with rules, canons, form and decorum, a unique musical artefact like *Messiah* would take time to establish itself with audiences and performers.

This is a tale of endurance, survival and ultimate triumph, marking the life-record of an outstanding work of art across two and a half centuries. Following Handel's death in 1759, *Messiah* soon became the victim of its own popularity, a cult object overshadowing the versatility and originality of the master's wider musical achievement in the field of opera, church music, chamber cantatas and instrumental compositions. Only during the twentieth century did a gradual recovery of the score as first conceived and performed bring its particular narrative to a kind of fortunate conclusion, which the sensibility of Handel's own age would have seen as entirely fitting. We are in a more advantageous position than our Victorian ancestors to appreciate the conceptual profundity and deftness of design entailed in Charles Jennens's 'scripture collection', and to admire the intense energy, idiomatic sophistication and imaginative focus with which Handel addressed himself to the task of setting this to music. I hope that this brief tribute to *Messiah*'s inherent robustness and integrity will encourage readers to listen to it—and take part in it—anew.

I

A COMPOSER AT THE CROSSROADS

By 1741, the year in which he composed *Messiah*, George Frideric Handel was a dominant figure on London's musical scene. Three decades earlier he had arrived as a visitor from his native Germany, presenting his opera *Rinaldo* at the Queen's Theatre in the Haymarket, writing a court ode for the birthday of Queen Anne and composing church music for official celebrations of the Peace of Utrecht, which ended the War of the Spanish Succession. His professional profile, that of a sophisticated foreign artist gifted in a variety of musical forms and styles, was quickly established and he saw obvious advantages in making London his permanent home. The capital had its own lively culture of music and theatre, sustained by increasing prosperity as a business centre with a stock market in which Handel himself would

become a shrewd investor. Geographically and socially, this eighteenth-century metropolis fell into two distinct zones: the City, where trading and banking took place, and, to the west, what was loosely called 'the Town', a fashionable, fast-expanding area of residential streets and squares surrounding the royal palace of St James's and containing the theatres in which so much of the composer's working life would be spent.

In its smartest quarter, on the edge of Hyde Park (then still rural, grazed by sheep and cows), Handel chose to settle in 1723, taking a house on an annual lease in the newly built Brook Street, close to the church of St George's, Hanover Square. The dedication of the church and the naming of the square were neither of them irrelevant to Handel's fortunes.

In 1714, when Queen Anne died, she was succeeded not, as some had hoped, by her exiled half-brother James Francis Edward Stuart, but by her cousin Georg Ludwig, Elector of Hanover, who ascended the British throne as King George I. This proved an obvious advantage to the composer, who had spent a brief period as music director (*Kapellmeister*) at the

OVERLEAF
Handel's music room in 25 Brook Street, Mayfair, where the composer made his home from 1723 until his death in 1759. The double-manual harpsichord is a modern copy of an eighteenth-century instrument by the Flemish firm of Ruckers.
CREDIT: © HANDEL HOUSE TRUST LTD

court in Hanover. He may indeed have combined his visits to London in 1710 and 1712 with information-gathering in relation to the succession issue. King George came from a music-loving family and Handel found himself commissioned to write church canticles for the Chapel Royal at St James's and to create what we now know as the *Water Music*, a sequence of airs and dance movements that accompanied a royal river excursion from Whitehall to Chelsea in the summer of 1717.

Hanover had its own opera house, so in London, at what was now the King's Theatre in the Haymarket, George I was happy to patronize a new enterprise, the so-called 'Royal Academy of Music', begun in 1719 as a seasonal subscription programme of operatic productions. His £1,000 contribution headed a distinguished list of subscribers, 'Persons of Honour' underwriting performances intended to reflect the highest available standards and production values in the world of international music theatre. Handel himself was commissioned to engage singers and orchestral musicians, and for the next twenty years the composition and presentation of opera would play a central role in his creative life.

Later ages tended to regard this extended stretch as a writer for the stage either as a kind of aesthetic wilderness in which Handel spent too long straying or as a drudgery from which he yearned to break free. Almost as soon as he died, in 1759, his operas—nearly forty of them in all—were forgotten, with the exception of a few arias in which generally innocuous English verses were substituted for their original Italian texts, more specific in expressing individual emotions such as triumph, rage, passionate yearning or erotic excitement. Only as of the late twentieth century has an astonishing revival of interest in these dramas, together with a viable approach to techniques of performance and staging for modern audiences, meant that such magnificent works as *Ariodante*, *Rodelinda*, *Giulio Cesare* and *Tamerlano* now enjoy a permanent place within the operatic repertoire throughout the world.

The beauties of line and craftsmanship we admire in Handel's operatic arias, together with their dramatic integrity in registering the feelings and motivations of the characters who sing them, were not universally admired by the audiences of his own day. He had to contend with the caprices of taste and fashion in Georgian London, and he was not always rewarded with loyalty or appreciation from the singers (mostly Italian and hired by the season) for whom he wrote new music or else adapted earlier numbers to suit their particular talents. In 1733, a rival undertaking, nowadays sometimes referred to as 'the Opera of the Nobility' from its foundation by a coterie of aristocrats, challenged Handel's ascendancy, introducing Londoners to newer operatic trends, and drawing both audiences and performers away from his theatre.

Handel's own management style, what was more, did him no favours. Dictatorial with his orchestra and impatient with the moods and whims of his singers, he was concerned to promote his own creations when it came to the choice of operas to be presented and showed relatively little interest in the work of contemporary composers, except where this offered inspiration for his own.

Though Handel continued writing and presenting operas throughout the 1730s, alternative musical forms were attracting his interest at the same time. In 1732, in response to pirate productions of the sacred drama *Esther* and the pastoral serenata *Acis and Galatea*, both written some fifteen years earlier for an aristocratic patron, he mounted his own performances of them, discovering in the process an enthusiastic audience for English-language dramatic works. The following year he carried this a stage further with the oratorios *Deborah* and *Athalia*, based on scriptural episodes from the Old Testament—bold experiments in full-length musical drama using English words. By the end of the decade Handel had fully consolidated on this creative project, deepening the narrative element embodied by the interaction of individual soloists through elaborately developed interventions from the chorus, functioning as a commentator on events or as a vehicle for moral and spiritual truths. Two of Handel's most epic explorations in this English oratorio territory he was steadily making his own came in 1738, with *Saul*, a work of monumental proportions featuring the largest orchestral forces he had so far employed, and, in the following year, *Israel in Egypt*. The descriptive sweep of

the latter's choruses remains unequalled by those written by any other composer for massed voices.

Whatever the professional zigzags of his career, Handel found time for friendship and socializing as an adoptive Londoner. He had become a naturalized Briton in 1727 but took care never to lose his German accent when speaking English or to abandon the essential cosmopolitanism of outlook and experience that gave him a perfect command of Italian and French and fuelled his polyglot musical style. He was an entertaining companion with a wide circle of acquaintances, which included aristocrats and members of the landed gentry, merchants, diplomats, affluent tradesmen and fellow musicians. They enjoyed his dry sense of humour, his gifts as a raconteur and his pleasure in fine pictures and good food. All of them were dedicated admirers of his music and kept each other informed about his latest works, whose rehearsals and first performances they were keen to attend, as well as purchasing the printed scores or having manuscript copies made for them.

OVERLEAF
Handel spent much of the 1720s and 1730s producing Italian operas for the London stage. This caricature of a performance of Handel's opera *Flavio* (1723) shows the Italian castrato Gaetano Berenstadt on the far right, the soprano Francesca Cuzzoni in the centre and the Italian castrato Senesino on the left.
CREDIT: WIKIMEDIA COMMONS

Such a powerful and compelling personality made its impact not just on this intimate circle, but on his patrons within the reigning Hanoverian dynasty, whose love of music guaranteed an enduring loyalty to the composer, strengthened by their shared German background.

King George I's successor, crowned as George II in 1727 to the sound of four elegantly contrasted anthems commissioned from Handel, remained a devoted supporter, appointing him music master to the royal children. The new king's consort, Queen Caroline, was equally enthusiastic, and it is hard not to see the magnificent elegy 'The ways of Zion do mourn', written for her funeral in 1737, as Handel's personal tribute to this cultured, discerning and strong-willed woman. The piece is another of those works from the late 1730s in which we see the composer extending his range within the choral medium and developing a new style for potential use in the oratorios on which he would focus in his last creative decade. Fusing court solemnity with wistful meditation and the kind of learned allusion to German church music of past generations that would have appealed to Caroline, the funeral anthem fully deserves its description by one of her daughters as 'ye finest cruel touching thing that ever was heard'.

Though he had not quite relinquished Italian opera as a core element in his career as a composer, there are plenty of indications, both in 'The ways of Zion do mourn' or the two oratorios *Saul* and *Israel in Egypt* written soon after it,

that Handel was in search of new inspirations and other musical forms in which to stretch his talent. The autumn of 1739 witnessed the first performance of his setting of John Dryden's 'Ode on St Cecilia's Day', a hymn of praise to the power of music, which must have held its own significance for Handel during this crucial period. At the same time he was at work on the set of twelve concertos for strings published as his Op. 6, a superbly ambitious achievement in which he exploits the concerto medium with greater imagination and audacity than had been shown by any other Baroque composer. No sooner were these completed than in February 1740 Handel produced one of his most astoundingly original works for voices and orchestra, the setting of John Milton's 'L'Allegro' and 'Il Penseroso', two poems that contrast such opposites as day and night, country and city, solitariness and conviviality, to which he added a balancing final section entitled 'Il Moderato', written by Charles Jennens, librettist of *Saul*. The entire piece, richly pictorial in its beguiling evocation of the rural scene, demonstrates Handel's consummate mastery of his musical resources, displaying a fund of inventiveness, which ought to have impressed his capricious London public somewhat more than it did at that particular moment.

Handel composes: a portrait by Philip Mercier dating from c. 1730, when Handel was in his mid-forties.
Credit: De Agostini Picture Library / A. Dagli Orti / Bridgeman Images

Even if, unlike most other musicians at this time, Handel did not rely mainly on regular employment from a princely patron or a religious institution, he was not free, correspondingly, of a need to anticipate the fluctuations of popular taste and to earn enough to ensure that his music was performed at the highest possible standard. The sheer pressure of work took its toll in the spring of 1737, with what a London newspaper reported as 'a Paraletick Disorder',[1] a stroke, which temporarily paralysed his right hand, needing a session at the curative thermal springs of Aachen in Germany before he recovered. His Italian operas meanwhile met with limited success and in January 1741 the last of these, *Deidamia*, a romantic comedy based on a Greek myth, was withdrawn after three performances.

Among the group of friends and musical enthusiasts surrounding him, where Handel would go from here was not obvious. A letter from an anonymous 'J. B.' in the London *Daily Post* for 4 April 1741 articulated their anxiety: 'If we are not careful for him, let us be for our own long-possessed Credit and Character in the polite world. If such a Pride be offended let us take it as the natural Foible of the great Genius, and let us overlook them like Spots upon the Sun.'[2] Had Handel, in short, exhausted the goodwill of London audiences and was he preparing to leave England for good?

Perhaps not immediately, but later that year an invitation arrived that gave him the perfect opportunity to get some much-needed distance from the metropolis in which he had spent the past thirty years as a creative artist, a working musician, an entrepreneur and entertainer. It was a request for him to visit Ireland and present a season of concert performances of his works in Dublin. This evidently came from the viceroy, William Cavendish, Duke of Devonshire, with support from various Irish charitable societies keen to raise funds after a series of disastrous harvests had brought poverty and starvation to communities across the country. In the autumn of 1741 Handel set off on the first leg of his journey, to Cheshire, where at Parkgate on the River Dee he boarded the packet boat for the voyage—fourteen hours with a fair wind—across the Irish Sea. Arriving in Dublin on 18 November he brought with him, among other scores, that of a new oratorio on which he had been working that August. It was called *Messiah*.

2

THE WORLD OF ORATORIO

What exactly is an oratorio and where does *Messiah* belong within this specialized musical genre? By the time Handel started composing his draft score in 1741, the oratorio form was well established throughout Europe, with different artistic styles determining its outlines in musical centres as far apart as Rome, Vienna, Hamburg and London. Handel himself had introduced it to English audiences during the late 1730s while continuing to produce Italian operas for the London stage, so that the narrative and dramatic aspects of each oratorio were influenced by his experiences as a theatre composer. Swiftly, however, his creative discourse pulled away from specifically operatic modes and structures to produce a more personal approach, as he started to develop the expressive possibilities of the chorus, both as commentator and participant in the musical drama.

Theatricality indeed—more specifically the dramatic impulse behind the Counter-Reformation—lay at the very roots of oratorio. The Italian word takes its name from the prayer meetings and spiritual exercises of a community of priests established in 1551 by the newly ordained Filippo Neri at the Roman church of San Girolamo della Carità. Here Filippo (later to be canonized) took over a little hall above the nave and this became a centre of religious activity for what eventually became the religious order of Oratorian Fathers. When in 1575 Pope Gregory XII gave them the bigger church of Santa Maria in Vallicella, the musical element in their worship became more elaborate, with extended dramatic texts, either in Latin or Italian, set to music that borrowed features from secular forms such as madrigal, solo song and recitative. Out of these miniature dramas grew the genre loosely known as 'oratorio', from its beginnings in St Filippo Neri's Roman oratory or prayer hall. While the Counter-Reformation aesthetic emphasized the significance in religious experience of rapture and ecstasy, which music so ideally helped to convey, there was no attempt made to stage oratorio as fully acted theatre, with costumes and sets. However, the exciting new musical genre known as 'opera' was emerging in Italy at exactly the same time and a natural cross-fertilization developed between the two forms. Composers adept at writing for the theatre were happy to write sacred dramas as well, and a skilful poet could turn his hand just as easily to a version of a Bible story for performance in front of an audience of priests or nuns as to a mythological or historical plot based on the erotic adventures of Greek heroes, Roman generals, nymphs or princesses. The same basic narrative instinct that brought Hercules, Julius Caesar, Ariadne or Agrippina onto the operatic stage gave dramatic substance to John the Baptist, St Cecilia, Abraham and Susanna. Between these two genres, what was more, the same singers could move with the greatest of ease. The early seventeenth century witnessed the rise of the dramatic castrato voice to a supremacy that would remain unchallenged for almost 200 years. Since the practice of castrating boys to produce adult male soprano and alto voices had become standard in the church choirs of the Counter-Reformation, it was desirable to cast them in female oratorio roles so as to avoid what was seen as the inappropriate participation of women in sacred performances of any kind.

Handel himself came across this problem of Catholic decorum while working in Rome in 1706–10. Under the patronage of influential and music-loving cardinals, he had made his first essay in the oratorio style with *Il trionfo del tempo e del disinganno* ('The Triumph of Time and Insight'),* a drama of personified abstracts in which Time, Truth and

* Thirty years later, in 1737, Handel revised and extended the work, giving it the title *Il trionfo del tempo e della verità* ('The Triumph of Time and Truth'). In 1757 the ailing Handel oversaw a further English-language revision.

Pleasure seek to engage the attentions of Beauty. This work, so arresting and imaginative, is really an extended dramatic cantata rather than an oratorio in the strictest sense, but its overall moral character belongs much more to a religious context than to the world of the stage. Rome, in any case, had no operatic activity at that period, owing to a papal ban on theatre performances, yet female singers were welcomed in the salons and music meetings of the aristocracy. One such artist was the young soprano Margherita Durastanti, whom Handel met during his residence in the household of Marchese Francesco Maria Ruspoli.

Under Ruspoli's patronage Handel composed a wealth of chamber cantatas, but in 1708 the Marchese commissioned him to write an oratorio on the theme of the Resurrection, to the poet Carlo Sigismondo Capeci's libretto, which sees Lucifer defeated through Christ's descent into hell as consolation is brought by St John to the mourning Mary Magdalen and Mary Cleophas. The *Oratorio per la resurrezione di Nostro Signor Gesù Cristo*, known as *La Resurrezione* in lists of Handel's works, was presented on a specially constructed stage in Palazzo Ruspoli, complete with lighting effects and ornate music stands for the orchestra, before an audience of 1,500 guests. In so far as this was not a fully dramatized performance, the Marchese observed the prevailing decorum but broke with it by casting Margherita Durastanti as Maria Maddalena. An infuriated Pope, Clement XI, administered a stern reproof to Ruspoli for daring to employ a woman in an Easter oratorio and threatened the soprano with a public flogging. Durastanti, however, was sufficiently well regarded by Handel to be given the title role in his opera *Agrippina*, premiered in Venice in 1709, and later to be asked to join his London company at the King's Theatre, Haymarket.

Opera was a relatively recent addition to London's cultural life when Handel first arrived there in 1710. Oratorio, on the other hand, was completely unknown in Britain, though seventeenth-century composers such as Henry Purcell and John Blow had written short musical episodes based on incidents in the Old and New Testaments. Handel's pioneering achievement in introducing English audiences to sacred lyric drama began with *Esther*, probably composed around 1718 for James Brydges, Duke of Chandos, revised in 1720, but then shelved for another twelve years until a revival at the Crown and Anchor Tavern in the Strand, to celebrate Handel's birthday. It made a powerful impression on its hearers. 'This oratoria [*sic*] or religious opera is exceeding fine', wrote one of them, 'and the company were highly pleased'.[1] Such a favourable reception encouraged Handel to make a further overhaul of the *Esther* score for performance at the King's Theatre in the Haymarket on 2 May 1732. While this featured singers from his Italian opera company, it was purely a concert performance, as a newspaper advertisement was concerned to point out: 'NB There will be no Action on the Stage, but the House will be fitted up in a decent Manner for the Audience, the Musick to be disposed after the Manner of the Coronation Service'.[2]

This non-theatrical presentation on a stage normally used for opera might have been due to the intervention of the Bishop of London, Edmund Gibson, anxious that chorus members from the Chapel Royal should not be distracted from their official duties. There is no evidence, however, to suggest that Handel wished to break free from the original concept of oratorio imparted to him while in Italy: that of a work whose musical language might be powerfully dramatic, using forms identical to those of opera, but which was not written for scenic representation by singing actors in costume. With *Esther*, a score to which he would often return in later years, the seed was planted at the King's Theatre for a valid alternative form of musical entertainment in London, patronized by many of those who bought tickets and subscriptions for the opera seasons, presenting works whose English texts allowed native talents to shine, rather than depending purely on the latest expensive Italian singing stars.

While Handel continued to write operas—among them *Ariodante*, *Alcina* and *Serse*, three of his most effective pieces for the stage—his phenomenal energy in the 1730s devoted itself equally to exploring the possibilities of an English oratorio form, which he had single-handedly brought into being. He was writing for an almost exclusively Protestant audience, so the stories of saints and martyrs favoured in

Italy, France and Austria were, in theory at least, not acceptable, and neither were the kind of allegorical dramas reinforcing points of religious dogma that were popular in Catholic clerical circles. 'Popery' was in any case deeply mistrusted throughout Britain, associated as it was with political intrigue on behalf of the Catholic Stuart dynasty and with international aggression on the part of France. The basis of popular Protestantism was a close study of the Bible, and it was narratives from the Old Testament that furnished Handel's English librettists, including Charles Jennens, with their subject matter.

In two such pieces, *Deborah* and *Athalia*, Handel took oratorio further in terms of expressive range and amplitude of design. The former, based on incidents from the Book of Judges, was hastily assembled as a pasticcio, a piece made up of numbers from other works (in this case Handel's own), but its epic grandeur of style made a real impact on the audience. This was substantially due to Handel's use of an expanded orchestra and his determination to make the chorus a key participant in the musical drama. *Athalia*, on the other hand, first performed at Oxford's Sheldonian Theatre as part of the university's end-of-year degree ceremonies, is a more intimate work, obliquely deriving from the Old Testament via a French play by Jean Racine, but here again the choral element becomes an essential motor of the action.

During the 1730s we watch Handel at work developing a specific English-language oratorio style, one that, while scrupulously observing the decorum of its audience's Protestantism, allows the composer to blend his unique choral discourse with the musical language of opera in the arias and recitatives. The intensely private world of Italian lyric drama, never involving more than half a dozen characters in its knotty scenarios of suffocating court or dynastic intrigue, now opens out into something simpler, more universal, with the chorus taking on the role of the wider community and the key relationship made spiritual rather than erotic. At the core of these sacred narratives lies the question of how such a community stands in relation to God and what it deserves at his hands. The same issue, expressed in terms of Christ's divinity, earthly suffering and resurrection, provides the inspiration for *Messiah*.

3

TO THE HIBERNIAN SHORE

Handel spent nearly a year in Ireland, almost all of this time in Dublin. The city, with a population of around 130,000, was one of the fastest-growing in Europe. As the centre of Irish government, it was dominated by a medieval castle, residence of an English-appointed viceroy, known as the Lord Lieutenant, and by the handsome colonnaded Parliament House built in 1729 to a design by the architect Edward Pearce. On College Green an equestrian statue of King William III reminded Dubliners that his victory over King James II at the Battle of the Boyne in 1690 had handed control of their country to a landholding Protestant oligarchy, governing the destinies of a Catholic majority. This powerful 'Ascendancy' finished off its sons' education at the exclusive Trinity College and worshipped at the city's two cathedrals of Christ Church and St Patrick's as members of the Anglican Church of Ireland. It was this Georgian Protestant echelon that left its enduring mark on Dublin in the shape of handsome brick-and-stucco streets and squares and on Ireland as a whole in a wealth of country houses. Though many of the latter were burned out during the struggle for Irish independence in the twentieth century, when a mixture of apathy, neglect and historic resentment of the Ascendancy also destroyed large areas of the Georgian metropolis, enough remains for visitors nowadays to absorb some of the environment Handel would have known during his stay in 1741–2.

The expanding city boasted an active dramatic culture at its two theatres in Smock Alley and Aungier Street, some of whose Irish actors, such as Peg Woffington, Kitty Clive and James Quin, became acquainted with Handel when they played in London. Equally vigorous was a musical life based on the resident Dublin Castle band employed by the Lord Lieutenant and known as the State Music. Consisting of fifteen players, this was led by the violinist Matthew Dubourg, a performer for whom Handel showed his esteem with a princely £100 bequest in his will. Among several outstanding pupils of the great Francesco Geminiani, Dubourg had settled in Dublin in 1721 and later became the State Music's official 'Master and Composer'. The poet Henry Carey wrote admiringly of him:

So fine a Genius, and so great a Hand,
Nature and Art (Dubourg) are at a stand:
On Thee they have bestow'd their riches Store:
Can we expect, or canst thou wish for more?

The State Music also featured the trumpeter William Clegg, whose son John, another noted violin virtuoso, joined the composer's London orchestra. Both before and after Handel's Irish visit, the two-way musical traffic brought Italian players to Dublin as well, including the renowned cellists Lorenzo Bocchi and Marc'Antonio Pasqualini, 'Pasqualino', who had taken part in the first performance of Handel's *Alexander's Feast* in 1736, and Francesco Geminiani, one of the era's greatest artists on the violin and a fine composer in his own right. No wonder an Irish clergyman foresaw the ruin of native music while

The Muses now from Albion's Isle retreat
And here with kind indulgence fix their seat.

Thus the Dublin audience could call itself a discerning one when it came to performance styles and standards, and Handel had considerable forces on which to draw for the six concerts he was now preparing at his lodgings in Abbey Street. For various works, including his new oratorio, he would require a more than adequate chorus, but this could be well supplied from among the cathedral choirs of Christ Church and St Patrick's. Dublin was already familiar with the Handel sound, since five years earlier, at St Andrew's Church, a benefit concert for one of the city's hospitals had featured his *Utrecht Te Deum and Jubilate* settings, together with one of the anthems he wrote for King George II's coronation. While there seems to have been some objection among Dublin's stricter Protestants to the so-called 'popish' aspects of oratorio, this did not deter Handel from pressing ahead with his programme. The fact that most of the items scheduled for inclusion, such as *L'Allegro, il Penseroso ed il Moderato* and *Acis and Galatea*, were not religious in character might have been the result of a warning to this effect from the Duke of Devonshire and others with whom he originally planned his Irish visit.

On 23 December 1741 the first of Handel's six projected concerts took place, featuring *L'Allegro, il Penseroso ed il Moderato* with three concertos. A correspondent in *Faulkner's Dublin Journal* noted 'a more numerous and polite Audience than was ever seen upon the like Occasion', adding that 'the Performance was superior to any Thing of the Kind in this Kingdom before; and our Nobility and Gentry, to show their Taste for all Kinds of Genius, expressed their great Satisfaction, and have already given all imaginable Encouragement to this grand Musick'.[1] The journalist's use of the term 'polite' is significant. In the eighteenth century the word carried far more weight than it does today, implying not just good manners, but a thorough acquaintance with the cultural aspirations, ideas and discourse of civilized society. In Dublin, as in London, Handel's audience was almost exclusively formed from the upper ranks of the metropolitan community, in this case the Protestant gentry and bourgeoisie as opposed to the 'native Irish', mostly Catholic and working class.

The venue for this and later concerts was a fine new music room whose existence no doubt provided another incentive for Handel's Irish venture. Opened in Fishamble Street, running down to the River Liffey from St Werburgh's Church, it had been built to a plan by Richard Cassel, a German soldier turned architect who had anglicized his name to Castle and made a sound reputation as a designer of town and country mansions for the Irish aristocracy. Only a single outer wall of this building now survives, so that apart from what can be gathered from a not especially good regency print, we know nothing of what it looked like. We can assume, however, that the spacious interior, seating around 600 people, contained a galleried auditorium with room for an orchestra and choir, but at this stage there was no organ. It could have been a larger version of the eighteenth-century Holywell Music Room in Oxford, a unique survival of this kind of music space from Handel's own era or soon after.

The Fishamble Street auditorium, 'finished in an elegant manner under the direction of Capt. Castle',[2] had been commissioned by Dublin's Charitable Musical Society, whose concerts were directly linked with a number of initiatives aimed at alleviating urban poverty within the rapidly growing city. The presence of 'Dr Handel, a Gentleman universally known by his excellent Compositions in all Kinds of Musick'[3] was an obvious selling point for the Charitable Musical Society, but the composer himself took time, once he had arrived, to assess the vocal and instrumental forces available to him before presenting his first concert. He was also awaiting the arrival of his featured soloists and busy selling subscriptions for the entire season. This, by the way, was an aspect of the composer's life we are often tempted to overlook. Much of the financial underpinning of his professional career depended on his own spirit of enterprise, so that his London house in Brook Street contained, not surprisingly, a room where tickets could be bought and copies of his scores purchased. Like many other musicians of his time, Handel was, as much as he needed to be, a businessman with an eye to his audience and its market potential. *Messiah*, like much else that he wrote, was part of an ongoing commercial venture, difficult though this might be for some of its modern admirers to accept.

In the midst of making his plans and arrangements for performances in the Fishamble Street music room, Handel seems to have found enough leisure for going into society, making himself agreeable to leading figures in Dublin, beginning with the Duke of Devonshire as Ireland's Lord Lieutenant. The amiable duke and his notoriously plain-speaking duchess were happy to patronize the concert season for motives that, it is plausibly suggested, were political as much as artistic. It was important for the duke, as the senior government official and representative of royal authority, to maintain the Irish parliament's support for Britain's ongoing wars with Spain and France. Hence a continuing programme of sophisticated entertainment during the winter months, with one of the most highly esteemed composers of the day at its centre, was calculated to keep everybody in the city whose votes and influence truly counted.

For Handel there was time to renew old acquaintances who for one reason or another had left London in earlier years. Chief among these was the author of the satirical *Gulliver's Travels*, Jonathan Swift, who had been appointed Dean of St Patrick's in 1713. The two men originally met in 1714, during the last days of Queen Anne's reign, when one of her doctors, John Arbuthnot, who had befriended Handel on his arrival in London, was a member of a writers' coterie known as the Scriblerus Club. Others in the group included Swift and the poets Alexander Pope and John Gay, both of whom contributed material to the texts of *Acis and Galatea* and the early oratorio *Esther*. Pope always maintained that he had no sensitivity at all to music, describing himself as possessing 'ears of an untoward make',[4] but he had a deep respect for Handel's overall achievement. This had been strengthened by their mutual friend Dr John Arbuthnot, who answered the poet's request for an expert assessment of Handel's talent simply by saying, 'Conceive the highest that you can of his abilities and they are much beyond anything you can conceive'.[5] Accordingly, when the composer departed for Ireland, Pope's imagination turned him into a heroic victim of the combined caprice, effeminacy and ignorance of London audiences, as part of *The Dunciad*, that devastating poetic satire on the contemporary cultural scene. The poet mocks the triumph of the Goddess of Dullness as he rails at mediocrity, money-grabbing and vulgarity in the world of the arts. In a footnote he blasts 'the false taste of playing tricks in Music with numberless divisions, to the neglect of that harmony which conforms to the Sense and applies to the Passions. Mr Handel had introduced a great number of Hands and more variety of instruments into the Orchestra, and employed even Drums and Cannon to make a fuller Chorus; which proved so much too manly for the fine Gentlemen of his age, that he was obliged to remove his Music into Ireland'.[6] The mention of 'Cannon' is a plain exaggeration, but Pope's noble rage on Handel's behalf can be felt in the lines of the poem itself:

But soon, ah soon, Rebellion will commence
If Music meanly borrows aid from Sense:
Strong in new Arms, lo! Giant Handel stands,
Like bold Briareus, with a hundred hands;
To stir, to rouse, to shake the Soul he comes,
And Jove's own Thunders follow Mars's Drums.

Arrest him, Empress, or you sleep no more—
She heard, and drove him to th'Hibernian shore.[7]

Jonathan Swift was another writer who claimed not to understand or appreciate music, yet clearly perceived the unique quality of Handel's artistic gifts and subsequently empathized with his more recent difficulties in making these acceptable to 'polite' audiences in England. Swift had been born in Ireland, but since his return there he had grown increasingly crotchety and eccentric. This was due partly to nervous illness and to the effects of a severe stroke, though many people by now believed he was half mad, driven to near-insanity, as it seemed, by disappointments in his career and a mounting disgust with his fellow human beings, that 'savage indignation' that the epitaph on his tomb in St Patrick's describes as tearing at his heart. Perhaps this explains Handel's initial reluctance to visit him, though when he finally paid a call, the servant who announced his name 'was a considerable Time e'er he could make the Dean understand him; which when he did, he cry's "Oh! A German and a Genius! A Prodigy! Admit him". The Servant did so, just to let Mr Handel behold the Ruins of the greatest Wit that ever lived among the Tide of Time'.[8]

By degrees Handel rallied his performers for the opening concerts of the season. A Dublin paper reported the arrival, in the Lord Lieutenant's yacht (faster than the packet boat), of 'Signiora Avolio, an excellent Singer, who is come to this Kingdom to perform in Mr Handel's Musical Entertainments'.[9] This was the Italian soprano Cristina Maria Avolio, of whose earlier career we know almost nothing, but who was evidently skilled enough to negotiate the trills and roulades of the virtuoso nightingale aria 'Sweet bird that shunn'st the noise of folly' in *L'Allegro, il Penseroso ed il Moderato* and to interpret the markedly contrasted roles of Galatea and Esther. As tenor soloist, Handel chose James Baileys, a member of the choir at both Christ Church and St Patrick's, who had sung, while in London, in the funeral anthem for Queen Caroline. His bass, John Mason, was another Dublin lay vicar, as was the counter-tenor Joseph Ward.

The most interesting addition of all to the soloists' line-up was one not originally planned by Handel. On 3 December 1741 there arrived in Dublin the young actress Susanna Maria Cibber.

She had been engaged originally by Handel's friend, the great Irish actor James Quin, to play at the Aungier Street theatre and came with a budding reputation as a tragedienne, which she would develop in a notable career on the London stage. Susanna's trip to Ireland, however, was not a

Susanna Maria Cibber arrived in Dublin in 1741 with a scandalous reputation, but proved a success when Handel chose her to be one of his singers for *Messiah*'s first performance. *CREDIT*: WIKIMEDIA COMMONS

purely professional move. In 1737 her husband, Theophilus Cibber, actor and company manager at Drury Lane, sought to sue one of her lovers, William Sloper, with whom he had hitherto complaisantly tolerated Susanna's ongoing liaison. Lurid details of the court case, which featured a snooping landlord, interconnecting bedrooms and an abduction attempt foiled at the last minute by her brother, the respected composer Thomas Augustine Arne, became the talk of London. Though Cibber received only £10 in damages (he had asked for £5,000), Susanna made a politic disappearance from London until James Quin coaxed her back to the stage via a season in Dublin. Thanks to Handel, her professional career was now about to take a new direction entirely.

4

ELEVATED, MAJESTIC AND MOVING

Once the Dublin concert season began, Handel might have been expected to feature *Messiah*, his newest oratorio, as part of the opening programme. There were several good reasons why he chose not to do so, two of them purely practical. As an accomplished showman, constantly alive to the quality and character of his audience, he would have been aware of his music's relative unfamiliarity among the listening public in the Irish capital. He needed to acclimatize their ears to his style and the world it created in sound before introducing them to an outright novelty. In addition, once he had gathered together his platform of soloists and assembled his chorus and orchestra, he would have to adapt his original autograph score so as to exploit these musical resources to maximum effect, taking their limitations into account. In the early weeks of 1742 there were adjustments to be made before the new work's premiere could be announced and suitably publicized to an audience that would have been able to form its own taste for Handel's music in the first subscription series.

This had been an immediate success. Writing to *Messiah*'s librettist Charles Jennens on 29 December 1741, Handel could boast that 'the Nobility did give me the Honour to make amongst themselves a Subscription for 6 Nights, which did fill a Room of 600 Persons, so that I needed not sell one single Ticket at the Door and without Vanity the Performance was received with a general Approbation'.[1] The Fishamble Street hall was decidedly to his liking: 'The Musick sounds delightfully in this charming Room, which puts me in such Spirits (and my Health being so good) that I exert myself on my Organ [presumably brought into the hall specially for the occasion] with more than usual success'.[2] Handel was also well aware of his listeners' social cachet: 'The Audience being composed (besides the Flower of Ladyes of Distinction and other People of the greatest Quality) of so many Bishops, Deans, Heads of the Colledg, the most eminent People in the Law as the Chancellor, Auditor General &c. . . . I cannot sufficiently express the kind treatment I receive here, but the Politeness of this generous Nation cannot be unknown to You, so I let You judge of the satisfaction I enjoy, passing my time with Honnour, profit and pleasure'.[3]

The atmosphere, we gather from all this, was very different from the London Handel had left behind, riven as it was with factions, snobbery and competitiveness. Encouraged by this positive reception, he was already planning to remain in Dublin after the season was over. As he told Jennens, 'They propose to have some more Performances when the 6 Nights of the Subscription are over, and My Lord Duc the Lord Lieutenant (who is allways present with all His Family on those Nights) will easily obtain a longer Permission for me by His Majesty, so that I shall be obliged to make my stay here longer than I thought'.[4] There was no obvious reason for him to hurry home once the subscription series was over, though the reference here to King George II underlines the value to Handel of the three pensions he received from the royal household and the corresponding need to clarify his position with the monarch, for whose family he was still a kind of *Kapellmeister*, however unofficial.

Amid the serene harmonies of this Dublin spring a single jarring note was sounded by no less a figure than Jonathan Swift himself. For the chorus in performances of *Esther* and *L'Allegro, il Penseroso ed il Moderato* featured in his concerts, Handel relied on singers from the cathedral choirs of Christ Church and St Patrick's, several of whom doubled for both churches, governed though each was by a separate dean and chapter. Both establishments were linked with the charitable initiatives that formed such a vital element in Dublin's civic society, and since Handel had demonstrated his readiness to give benefit performances in aid of the various charities, it seemed reasonable for the senior clergy to allow their lay vicars and choristers to take part.

Suddenly and disastrously, however, this turned out not to be the view of the half-crazed dean of St Patrick's. 'Whereas it hath been reported', thundered Swift in a letter to his sub-dean, Dr Wynne, 'that I gave a license to certain vicars to assist at a club of fiddlers in Fishamble Street, I do hereby declare that I remember no such license to have been ever signed or sealed by me; and that if ever such pretended license should be produced, I do hereby annul and vacate the said license; intreating my said Sub-Dean and Chapter to punish such vicars as shall ever appear there, as songsters, fiddlers, pipers, trumpeters, drummers, drum-majors or in any sonal quality, according to the flagitious aggravations of their respective disobedience, rebellion, perfidy and ingratitude'.[5] To say that Swift was overstating the case would be putting it mildly, and since this letter is extant only in draft it might well not have been sent at all. There is a distinct possibility, on the other hand, given the dean's unique sense of humour, that he might have meant the whole thing as a joke at the choir's expense. Whatever the truth, someone—perhaps Handel himself—interceded for the choir, and in any case Swift was soon to be relieved of his clerical responsibilities on the grounds of mental decay.

During February and March of 1742 Handel was kept busy, both with making the necessary adjustments to the score of *Messiah* for its eventual premiere and with entertaining his Dublin audience as composer and performer. The power of the Handel sound over his Irish listeners was enhanced by the presence of Matthew Dubourg as his orchestral concertmaster, though on one occasion the great violinist got rather too carried away. 'One night, while Handel was in Dublin', Charles Burney tells us, 'Dubourg having a solo part in a song and a close to make *ad libitum*, he wandered about in different keys a great while, and seemed indeed a little bewildered and uncertain of his original, but at length, coming to the shake [trill] which was to terminate this long close, Handel, to the great delight of the audience, and augmentation of applause, cried out loud enough to be heard in the most remote parts of the theatre, "You are welcome home, Mr Dubourg"'.[6]

Around this time, it seems, Handel made the decision to include Susanna Cibber among his singers, having heard her in her brother Thomas Arne's *Comus* at the theatre in Aungier Street. Whatever relationship developed between the young actress, so recently bruised by her experience in the London law courts, and the elderly composer, himself no stranger to slander and hostility, was entirely professional, a working friendship rather than anything more intimate, yet profitable in its way to each of them. Handel evidently admired and encouraged Susanna's talent as an expressive singer, whose grasp of emotion and meaning in the text made up for her vocal limitations. She in her turn would have been grateful for the way in which their association,

'The Musick sounds delightfully in this charming Room'. The music room in Fishamble Street, Dublin, venue for the first performance of *Messiah*. *CREDIT*: HULTON ARCHIVE / GETTY IMAGES

now beginning in Dublin, enabled her to return at length to the London stage and recommence her career.

The excitement created by Handel's continuing presence in Ireland was sustained by patronage from Dublin Castle. His January 1742 concerts were advertised as 'By their Graces the Duke and Duchess of Devonshire's special Command', which might tempt us to discount efforts by modern Handel scholars[7] to underplay the duke's role in personally inviting the composer to Ireland. That he had indeed done so was stated for a fact by the Irish poet Laurence Whyte in verses on 'the General Effect and excellency of Musick, particularly on the famous Mr Handel's performance, who had been lately invited into this Kingdom by his Grace the Duke of Devonshire . . . for the Entertainment of Nobility and Gentry'. Whyte's long, not especially distinguished poem, summoning Irish bards 'to waken from your downy pillows', extols the duke's benign viceregal rule, singling out for special praise his invitation to 'our German Orpheus'. Earnestly hamfisted attempts at analysing Handel's musical effects and his keyboard technique on 'the Organ or the trembling Wire [the harpsichord]' conclude with a section headed 'Corollaries', celebrating the universal power of music as the creator of 'Our Peace and Concord, Liberty and Law'. Whyte's closing lines bring Devonshire before us once again, this time as the benefactor who

our Sorrows to allay
Invites the Nation to hear Handel play.[8]

On 24 March 'the Nation'—a small and select portion of it at any rate—heard Susanna Cibber make her debut for the composer in a version of his opera *Imeneo*, which, having recently failed in London, was now adapted for concert performance and fared rather better. Meanwhile *Faulkner's Dublin Journal* carried the following momentous announcement: 'For Relief of Prisoners in the several Gaols, and for the Support of Mercer's Hospital in Stephen's Street, and of the Charitable Infirmary on the Inns Quay, on Monday 12 April will be performed at the Music Hall in Fishamble Street, Mr Handel's new Grand Oratorio, call'd the MESSIAH'.[9] Tickets cost half a guinea—ten shillings and sixpence—and with them came free entry to a morning rehearsal on 9 April. This latter fulfilled all expectations: 'A most Grand, Polite and crouded Audience' heard 'Mr Handell's new Grand Sacred Oratorio . . . performed so well, that it gave universal Satisfaction to all present, and was allowed by the greatest Judges to be the finest Composition of Musick that ever was heard'.[10]

Partly because of Mrs Cibber's Aungier Street commitments, but possibly also because Handel needed to make last-minute changes to the score, the premiere was moved from 12 to 13 April. Another paper, the *Dublin News-Letter*, commenting on the rehearsal, had noted that 'the elegant Entertainment was conducted in the most regular manner',[11] suggesting that the audience had managed to behave itself rather better than usual. The eighteenth-century public, 'grand' or 'polite' though it might appear, was not always as civil once inside the theatre as it liked to think, and there was often a good deal of barging, jostling and pushing on staircases, in corridors or among the rows of benches in the pit. Space was always at a premium and at this eagerly awaited premiere the stewards of the Charitable Music Society spotted likely difficulties created by the fashionable hooped skirts worn by female audience members. To a request 'that the Ladies who honour this Performance with their Presence would be pleased to come without Hoops, as it will greatly increase the Charity, by making Room for more company' they added another, 'that the Gentlemen are desired to come without their Swords'.[12] The latter were nowadays merely a fashion accessory. Handel himself, who in his younger days once fought a duel with a fellow composer, sports a sword in his swagger portrait by Thomas Hudson, but in a crowded music room such an accoutrement would only make for further obstruction.

Without their hoops and swords, the *beau monde* of Dublin thronged Fishamble Street on the evening of 13 April 1742 for the first performance of Handel's *Messiah*. 'Words are wanting', wrote the anonymous correspondent for *Faulkner's Dublin Journal*, 'to express the exquisite Delight it afforded to the admiring crouded Audience'. In his next sentence the same writer devises what is surely the finest encapsulation of the oratorio's impact on generations of listeners ever since: 'The Sublime, the Grand and the Tender, adapted to the most elevated, majestic and moving Words, conspired to transport and charm the ravished Heart and Ear'. Handel and his singers Cristina Avolio and Susanna Cibber, together with the orchestra's leader Matthew Dubourg, had all given their fees for the evening to the three good causes advertised, 'satisfied with the deserved Applause of the Publick and the conscious Pleasure of promoting such useful and extensive Charity'.[13] In all, the takings for that momentous first night amounted to £400—over £51,000 in modern money.

Two audience reactions to *Messiah* performances in Dublin are worth noting. One was the response of Dr Patrick Delany, Chancellor of St Patrick's Cathedral, to the interpretation by Mrs Cibber of the aria 'He was despised'. Dr Delany was a great friend of Jonathan Swift and himself a poet of some talent, who later married Handel's neighbour, Mary Pendarves, part of a circle of London enthusiasts and admirers of the composer who kept each other well informed as to his newest works, his state of health and (sometimes) his eccentric behaviour. Delany himself was noted for

The title page of the printed wordbook for the Dublin performance of *Messiah*, April 1742.
CREDIT: © THE GERALD COKE HANDEL FOUNDATION, THE FOUNDLING MUSEUM, LONDON

The
Most Celebrated
SONGS
in the
ORATORIO
call'd
QUEEN ESTHER
To which is Prefixt
The Overture *in* Score
Compos'd by
Mr. Handel.

London. Printed for & Sold by I. Walsh Musick Printer & Instrument-maker to his Majesty at the Harp & Hoboy in Catherine Street in the Strand his compassion and sensitivity, so such an intense reaction to Susanna Cibber's singing could be seen on this occasion as altogether typical of him. Her scandalous reputation had preceded her to Dublin, which explains why he chose to express his admiration not merely by rising from his seat, but by quoting Christ's words to the woman taken in adultery: 'Woman, for this be all thy sins forgiven thee'.[14]

The other takes the form of some penetrating remarks on the oratorio by Edward Synge, Bishop of Elphin, which Handel sent on to Charles Jennens. The work, observed the bishop, 'seems to be a Species of Musick different from any other, and this is particularly remarkable of it. That tho' the Composition is very Masterly & artificial, yet the Harmony is So great and open, as to please all who have Ears & will hear, learned & unlearn'd'. Synge had watched the other audience members carefully: 'They seem'd indeed thoroughly engaged from one end to the other. And to their great honour, tho' the young & gay of both Sexes were present in great numbers, their behaviour was uniformly grave and decent, which Show'd that they were not only pleas'd but affected with the performance'.[15] Was it only the music in *Messiah* that made them 'grave and decent' and held their attention 'from one end to the other'? How closely did they follow the discourse of its biblical text?

To

Charles Jennens Esqr Junior

at Gopsal near Atherstone

Coventry bag —

6

5

THE MYSTERIOUS MR JENNENS

Musicians in the eighteenth century were experienced travellers, prepared to cover immense distances along rutted, muddy and dangerous roads in carriages or on horseback, to make hazardous crossings over mountains, seas and rivers and to acquire alien languages, customs and lifestyles, all in the cause of finding profitable employment. They learned to face the hardship of lengthy separations from family and friends and taught themselves not to miss the places they called home too deeply. As a result of these journeys, the music they composed or performed often needed to be adaptable to circumstance, material that could be easily packed and carried, with a view to adjusting it to whatever resources were available at the destination.

London Sept. 9th. 1742.

Dear Sr

It was indeed Your humble Servant which intended You a visit in my way from Ireland to London, for I certainly could have given You a better Account by word of mouth, as by writing, how well Your Messiah was received in that Country, yet as a Noble Lord, and no less then the Bishop of Elphin (a Nobleman very learned in Musick) has given his observations in writing of this Oratorio, I send you here annexed the contents of it in his own words. —
I shall send the printed Book of the Messiah to Mr Steel for You.
As for my success in General in that generous and polite Nation, I reserve the account of it till I have the Honour to see You in London.
The report that the Direction of the Opera next winter is comitted to my Care, is groundless. The gentlemen who have undertaken to middle with Harmony can not agree, and are quite in a Confusion. Whether I shall do some thing in the Oratorio way (as several of my friends desire) I can not determine as yet. Certain it is that this time 12 month I shall continue my Oratorio's in Ireland, where they are a going to make a large subscription allready for that Purpose. —
If I had known that My Lord Guernsey was so near when I

It does not lessen Handel's achievement in any way to say that *Messiah* was a work of exactly this portable kind. He had not composed it expressly for performance in Dublin, but evidently he realized how this new oratorio might be accommodated within his intended concert programme, so once settled in his Abbey Street lodgings, he started making the necessary alterations to the score. His immediate impact on musical Dubliners offered a further encouragement towards giving *Messiah* its first hearing in the Fishamble Street music room. The space was a congenial test-bed for the new piece and it also gave Handel, always conscious of his status as a gentleman, the chance to return 'the Politeness of this generous Nation'[1] with due style and generosity.

The letter of 29 December 1741 in which Handel used this phrase was addressed to Charles Jennens, collator and arranger of the biblical texts that make up *Messiah*'s libretto. From several important aspects the oratorio belongs as much to its author as to its composer. In terms of overall

OVERLEAF
A letter from Handel to his librettist Charles Jennens, 9 September 1742. The composer enclosed with the letter a written account of the first performance of *Messiah* by 'no less than the Bishop of Elphin (A Nobleman very learned in musick)', and promised to 'send the printed Book of the Messiah to Mr Sted' on behalf of Jennens.

design, outline and intention, nothing like it had ever been heard before, either in Britain or in continental Europe. Oratorios, as we have seen, were traditionally narrative in form, based on the lives and exploits of saints, martyrs or figures from the Old and New Testaments. Now and then they focused on personified abstracts—Divine Love, Christian Faith, Envy, Pride—who interacted with the human characters in the story. While *Messiah*'s three 'acts' form a distinctive theological sequence,* the work is exclusively non-dramatic in terms of its text, even if Handel seized every opportunity for theatrical nuance in his musical handling of the various scriptural verses.

We need to take a closer look now at Charles Jennens himself, whose original concept *Messiah* was, and whose involvement with Handel—as an admirer of his music, a librettist, patron and critic—occupied such a vital role in the composer's life during its most significant later phases. The two men played to one another's strengths while unashamedly exploiting such talents at the same time. Handel, calculating and opportunistic whenever it should suit him, knew, as is clear from the tone of his surviving letters to Jennens, how to lay on the deference and respect that his correspondent would have considered his due. Jennens on the other hand was happy to use Handel's music as a vehicle

* See Appendix II.

for his own frequently subversive political and religious agenda.

In terms of Georgian England's hidebound social stratification, Charles Jennens was not quite the gentleman he appeared. 'I was born and bred in Leicestershire mud',[2] he once jokingly observed to a friend, alluding to his splendid house in that county, Gopsall Hall. In origin, however, the Jennens family were distinctly 'new money', most of which had been made from iron manufacture in Birmingham, which was already a noted centre of heavy industry and engineering. Jennens himself was rich enough to be able to live in princely style both at Gopsall, with its Palladian porticoes and magnificent sweep of parkland, and at a fine London house in Great Ormond Street, where he spent part of the year enjoying the opera, oratorio and concert season in the company of music-loving friends.

A bachelor, sensitive, shy and given to moments of intense introspection, he was described as having 'a delicate Texture of the nervous System, too liable to Irritation; from whence arise violent Perturbations and Anxieties of the Mind, and not infrequently an extreme Lowness and Depression of the Spirits'.[3] Perhaps this was what attracted Jennens

'I was born and bred in Leicestershire mud'. Charles Jennens of Gopsall Hall, as portrayed by Thomas Hudson in the 1740s. *CREDIT*: © HANDEL HOUSE TRUST LTD

to the biblical story of King Saul, as told in the First Book of Samuel, on which he based an outstanding dramatic libretto for Handel to set. First produced in 1739, *Saul* is the loftiest, most amply proportioned of the composer's oratorios, and we can sense Handel's genuine excitement at first encountering Jennens's cleverly varied, fast-paced handling of the powerful narrative, centred on King Saul's tragically flawed personality and his obsessive jealousy of the heroic David. The composer and librettist would resume their collaboration the following year, when Jennens, having acted as editor of a version of Milton's 'L'Allegro' and 'Il Penseroso', prepared for Handel by their mutual friend James Harris, supplied a concluding section designed to balance the two, written in passable Miltonic pastiche and entitled 'Il Moderato'.

Jennens was an ardent collector of musical scores, many of them acquired and sent to him by his great friend Edward Holdsworth while travelling in Italy as a tutor—or 'bear-leader' as such preceptors were known—to young English noblemen making the Grand Tour. Comparatively little music in those days found its way into print (only a limited number of Handel's own works was actually published during his lifetime), and most of Jennens's score library was in manuscript form. Several volumes were lent to Handel, who could thus indulge his usual habit of borrowing snatches of music by other masters to embellish his own. Jennens was wise to such thefts. In a letter to Holdsworth dated 17 January 1743, acknowledging receipt of a packet of Italian scores, he notes sardonically that 'Handel has borrow'd a dozen of the Pieces & I dare say I shall catch him stealing from them, as I have formerly'.[4]

His regard for the composer was unaffected by this—a modern biographer calls him 'a self-confessed Handel addict'.[5] Jennens's devotion to Handel's music was of the sort that enjoys having the scores to hand just as much as listening to them in performance. He had subscribed to published editions of the operas during the 1720s and soon began assembling his own library of manuscript copies of Handel's works. Around 1740, just before the pair of them embarked on their *Messiah* project, Jennens appears to have started gathering together an entire set of his favourite musical master's available output, in the form of carefully prepared manuscript scores from Handel's own team of musical copyists, which he could then edit, if need be, with his usual meticulousness, adding details, notes and corrections as he went through them. This personal collection, emblematic both of Jennens's lifelong enthusiasm and of the absolute steadfastness of his regard for Handel, whatever their occasional differences, was bequeathed to a relative, Lord Aylesford, and most of the material is now in the Central Public Library in Manchester.

Music, as often happens, played a major role in lifting Jennens out of troughs of depression. Perhaps he felt an affinity, in this respect, with King Saul, whose story of melancholy soothed by music he had dramatized so brilliantly for Handel. The opportunity to have his own words set by his favourite composer was eagerly embraced. There was, however, another reason altogether why Handel's genius offered him such comfort, but this was as much political as artistic. Jennens was a non-juror, one of a minority who could not accept the succession, in 1714, of the Elector of Hanover to the British crown as King George I. Remaining loyal to the exiled royal House of Stuart, non-jurors felt unable conscientiously to swear any oath of service to a monarch they regarded as a usurper—the Latin *jurare* means 'to swear', hence 'non-juror'. This principle remained firm among them under his successor King George II, thus non-jurors did not allow themselves to take a full part in the public life of eighteenth-century England, since such gentlemanly professions as the army and navy, the magistracy and civil service all understood 'the King' in an oath of allegiance to mean the current head of the House of Hanover.

That Handel received pensions and employment from the Hanoverians and was plainly untroubled in his loyalty to them was a reality perhaps made easier for Jennens by the fact that the composer was himself of German origin. As for Jennens's politics, these do not seem to have alarmed Handel, even if perhaps a mutual awareness of their differences in this respect helped to sharpen the edges of their social and personal relationship. What emerges from the artistic collaboration between the two men is Handel's continuing usefulness to Jennens in promoting the latter's political ideology. *Saul*, for example, dramatizes the replacement of one king by another and at the close of the oratorio we hear David execrate the killing of Saul by the unnamed Amalekite as sacrilege against 'the anointed of the Lord'. In a later oratorio, *Belshazzar* (1745), Jennens plainly establishes a parallel between the restoration of the Jews to their homeland and the return of the Stuarts so ardently desired by non-jurors but not yet a reality.

Jennens's typically thoughtful, agonized approach to such issues was linked to his own religious outlook. Directly from his profound Anglican commitment springs *Messiah*, a work that, like *Saul* and *Belshazzar*, carries within it a subtext reflecting ideas that, for different reasons, he preferred to propagate through the medium of oratorio rather than communicate overtly. Non-jurors, after all, were Jacobites, the name originally given to those who had supported the cause of King James II (Latin *Jacobus*) on his self-imposed exile in 1688 during the so-called 'Glorious Revolution'. James, while himself a fervent and proselytizing Roman Catholic, was nominally supreme governor of the Church of England, a paradox that exacerbated the crisis of loyalty experienced by Protestant non-jurors. Charles Jennens was one of these, his Protestantism as deeply rooted as his devotion to the Stuart dynasty. At Gopsall Hall he built a splendidly appointed chapel for himself and his household (or 'family', to use the eighteenth-century expression) with cedar-wood panelling, an ornate reading desk and delicate stucco ceiling decoration. As befitted a non-juror, the communion table was partially made from a branch of the oak tree in which King Charles II had hidden during his escape following the battle of Worcester, while the prayer books had the names of the Hanoverian royal family removed wherever these might occur.

Jennens's own theology went much further than this sort of cosmetic deletion and directly determined the slant of *Messiah*'s underlying spirituality. Conservatism for non-jurors was a state of mind, which directed more than just their politics. By the 1740s, the decade of the oratorio's composition and earliest performances, the impact of the scientific revolution begun in the previous century was starting to erode the traditional basis of religious belief. Doubt, scepticism and cynicism assailed Christianity as the Enlightenment took hold and the established churches, whether in Protestant England or the Catholic realms of Western Europe, found their doctrines rejected and faced an unprecedented challenge to their position as agents of social control.

Even if 'Il Moderato', his addition to 'L'Allegro' and 'Il Penseroso', can speak of 'Reason's Empire . . . restoring intellectual day', Jennens was emphatically not a child of the Age of Reason when it came to matters of faith. Like most of those who shared his opinions on the contentious issue of dynastic succession to the British crown, he cherished a belief system based on the concept of mystery and revelation, at the centre of which stood the figure of Christ the Redeemer, wondrously resurrected from the tomb and promising an equal triumph over death to all who truly acknowledged Him. Central to this personal creed—and central therefore to *Messiah*—is the concept of a God 'who giveth us the victory through our Lord Jesus Christ', implicitly rejecting all notions of reasoned dispute as a foundation for faith and asserting the centrality of a miraculous Resurrection.

'Everything that has been united with Handel's music', Jennens once remarked, 'becomes sacred by such a union in my eyes'.[6] How long exactly he had contemplated uniting his favourite composer's music with holy scripture we cannot know, but by the summer of 1741 he had assembled (and in certain places adapted) those Old and New Testament texts that formed the core of his own religion. As he told Edward Holdsworth on 10 July, 'Handel says he will do nothing next Winter, but I hope I shall perswade him to set another Scripture Collection I have made for him & to perform it for his own Benefit in Passion Week'.[7] Was the earlier 'Scripture Collection' implied here the oratorio *Israel in Egypt*, based entirely on biblical passages and first performed in April 1739?

Perhaps, though for that work Handel might have assembled the text on his own initiative. To the present project, nevertheless, Jennens attached a particular significance: 'I hope he will lay out his whole genius & Skill upon it, that the Composition may excell all his former Compositions, as the Subject excells every other Subject. The Subject is Messiah'.[8]

6

THE LORD GAVE THE WORD

In arranging his 'Scripture Collection' for Handel to set, Jennens would have been aware of the composer's own knowledge of the Bible, demonstrated in earlier works such as the funeral anthem for Queen Caroline, the anthems written for James Brydges, Duke of Chandos, and those provided for King George II's coronation in 1727. On that occasion, when some of the senior clergy due to take part in the ceremony presumed to indicate various texts Handel might care to choose, he apparently 'murmured and took offence, as he thought it implied his ignorance of Holy Scriptures: "I have read my Bible very well and shall chuse for myself"'.[1] He came, after all, from a devoutly Protestant family. During the Thirty Years War his paternal grandparents had moved from predominantly Catholic Breslau (now the Polish city of Wrocław) to the more tolerant religious climate of Halle in Saxony. His mother Dorothea Taust was the daughter of a Lutheran pastor whose own family had also been religious refugees 'for love of the pure evangelical truth'.[2] Handel himself, once he had settled in London, was a regular worshipper at the church of St George's, Hanover Square. Even if not necessarily inclined, like Charles Jennens, to ponder weighty questions of theology, Handel was perfectly able to look his librettist in the face when it came to both a reverence for the scriptures and an understanding of the Christian message that they enshrined.

Whatever the gravity and portentousness of its sacred text, *Messiah* was nevertheless designed from the outset as a work for performance in a secular context, an oratorio as the term was understood by eighteenth-century London theatre audiences. The Dublin journalist's reference to it as an 'Entertainment' is crucial, but we need to detach this word from its modern nuances associated with comedy, song-and-dance and a generally superficial level of popular amusement. Audiences in Handel's time were 'entertained' by everything from a tragedy or an opera to recitations of Greek and Latin poetry or even a church sermon. Jennens himself later took up the expression when writing of 'a collection I gave Handel, call'd Messiah, which I value highly, & he has made a fine Entertainment of it'.[3] English oratorio entertained its audience in a form with which many of them were already familiar, the three-act structure traditionally employed by Italian operas of the kind Handel presented at theatres in the Haymarket, Covent Garden and Lincoln's Inn Fields. His friend Newburgh Hamilton, who had arranged Dryden's poem 'Alexander's Feast' as an ode for Handel to set and later developed the libretto of *Samson* from Milton's 'Samson Agonistes', called oratorio 'a musical Drama, whose Subject must be Scriptural, and in which the Solemnity of Church-Musick is agreeably united with the most pleasing Airs of the Stage'.[4] This was the basic principle on which Jennens planned his *Messiah* text, though the potency of the work as a whole derives as much from the ways in which it differs from this established model as from its observance of the customary parameters.

The latter become more obvious through the piece's division into three parts, an arrangement made clear by the wordbook Jennens prepared for the first London performance of *Messiah* at Covent Garden in 1743. Part I focuses on the prophecies made by Isaiah, Haggai and Malachi as to the advent of the Messiah, the effect of this on humankind—'Who may abide the day of his coming? And who shall stand when he appeareth?'—and the Virgin Birth. The single Nativity incident included, the moment at which the Angel announces Christ's birth to the shepherds, is intended to reinforce the concept of the Incarnation as a divine mystery before the final section of this opening act introduces the theme of Jesus as miracle-worker and redeemer foretold by the Old Testament prophets.

For his second act Jennens devised a striking change of mood. Here we meditate on Christ's Passion, his scourging—'wounded for our Transgressions . . . bruised for our Iniquities'—and the agonies of the Crucifixion, more especially the mockery and lack of compassion among the bystanders. The Resurrection and Ascension are evoked in the chorus 'Lift up your heads' and the air 'Thou art gone up on high', after which follows the drama of Whit Sunday, when the apostles become messengers of God's word, triumphing at last over its initial rejection by the mighty of the earth. It is at this point that *Messiah*'s best-known musical number, the 'Hallelujah' chorus, appositely clinches the overall message of the Christian narrative: that of victory achieved by way of suffering.

How Christ's experience encompasses the whole of humanity is the subject of Part III, which dwells on the universal promise of eternal life, the conquest of sin and death, the resurrection of the body (as affirmed in the Creed) and the praises due to Christ as 'the Lamb that was slain, and hath redeemed us to God by his blood'. In a sense, what we witness here is the resolution of that theological paradox central to Christian teaching—'We shall not all sleep, but we shall all be changed, in a Moment, in the Twinkling of an Eye'—the idea that death, so far from being a total extinction, represents a process of awakening to new life beyond the grave. Jennens's consummately skilful ordering of his scriptural verses, in such a way as to suggest that the

Saviour's earthly existence as set forth in the Gospels fulfils the visions of the prophets, emphasizes that 'Mystery of Godliness' referred to by St Paul in his First Epistle to Timothy. On the title page of his *Messiah* wordbook, together with a quotation from Virgil, *'Majora canamus'* ('Let us sing of greater things'), taken from a poem commonly held to foreshadow Christ's birth, this Pauline verse encapsulates the whole theme of the oratorio. In full it runs as follows: 'And without Controversy, great is the Mystery of Godliness: God was manifested in the Flesh, justified in the Spirit, seen of Angels, preached among the Gentiles, believed on in the World, received up into Glory. In whom are hid all the Treasures of Wisdom and Knowledge'.

We can see exactly why Jennens should have chosen this as a suitable epigraph. The text, as well as conveying a sense of incontrovertible assertion in its succinct summary of the Christian thesis, uses certain words and phrases, which, by their very nature, implicitly reject the reasonable approach to religion currently being adopted by the Enlightenment. 'Without Controversy' and 'justified in the Spirit, seen of Angels' are defiant in the face of philosophical rationalism, while ideas of concealment and mystery in Pauline teaching enhance the significance of revelation as an essential reward of steadfast faith, challenging any notion that the Word of God should be made subject to merciless intellectual scrutiny. The supernatural and suprarational, in Jennens's spiritual world view, offer a supreme justification for belief.

With their nicely judged calibrations of scriptural material, some of it, such as 'I know that my Redeemer liveth', blended from discrete Old and New Testament sources, the three parts of *Messiah* needed further division if the work as a whole was to function adequately as an oratorio on the London stage. Non-theatrical as the work might appear (and as such, indeed, was meant to appear), it is, as one modern authority states, 'for all its lack of stated plot, a drama, though one in which the momentum is primarily internal and intellectual rather than external'.[5] Jennens's librettos for *Saul* and *Belshazzar* show us how vividly his dramatic imagination could work. Not for nothing was he a pioneering editor of Shakespeare's plays. Scenes such as Saul's heart-wrenching encounter with the Witch of Endor and the thrilling 'Writing on the Wall' episode possess a vigorously stage-worthy quality, which has helped, in modern times, to bring both oratorios into the theatre.

Thus *Messiah* assumed, from its conception, a number of important dramatic aspects. Its original audiences, accustomed to the conventional fortunate conclusion of most Italian operas, even those with the most sombre and tragically inflected plots, would have appreciated the upbeat finale of Part III. The very nature of the Christian narrative, after all, is to arrive at the same kind of *lieto fine* ('happy end') as those of *Rodelinda*, *Giulio Cesare* or *Ariodante*, in each of which the characters have to undergo near-death ordeals in order to obtain contentment. They would have enjoyed the opportunities it offered Handel for deploying a self-consciously theatrical style in airs including 'Why do the nations so furiously rage together', 'Rejoice greatly, O daughter of Zion' or 'How beautiful are the feet of them', and they would have grasped the appropriateness of placing the oratorio's only duet, 'Oh death, where is thy sting?', just before the close of Part III, exactly that place in the score where, in so many of Handel's Italian operas, the voices of the hero and heroine are permitted to blend at last.

What Jennens grasped from the outset, in preparing *Messiah* for Handel's musical treatment, was the need to assign the individual scriptural extracts to their various functions as arias, choruses and recitatives. The Baroque musical tradition inherited and consolidated by Handel conceived its large-scale vocal works in terms of closed numbers, whose opening and culminating periods made themselves perfectly clear through the nature of their musical setting. These items were linked, in opera and oratorio, by stretches of recitative, either with a simple accompaniment from continuo instruments or else punctuated by chords from the orchestra, the latter mostly used to heighten moments of particular emotional or dramatic significance. Jennens would also have been aware in thus dividing his text that some, if not all, of its interpreters were likely to be drawn from among singers with proven theatrical experience, much of it gained on the operatic stage.

As it happened, Handel chose when setting *Messiah* to avoid giving his soloists too many obvious opportunities to exhibit the kind of virtuosity favoured by the star castrati and prima donnas for whom he had provided bravura arias during his years in the theatre. Only three of the solo airs possess the middle section and *da capo* repeat customary in the Italian lyric drama of the time and sometimes carried over into oratorio.* Handel was already putting this most artificial of closed forms behind him and its inclusion, except at certain key moments such as the bass's 'The trumpet shall sound', must in any case have seemed inappropriate to the nature of the oratorio as he and Jennens respectively understood it. He was economical, what is more, with his recitatives. As Bishop Synge pointed out, there is no dialogue in the piece, so the need for accompanied speech is restricted to moments when a new subject has to be introduced. Even those recitatives carried by the string orchestra often assume an *arioso* character, the tenor's opening 'Comfort ye, my people' being a case in point. Here as elsewhere in *Messiah* we can sense Handel's intuitive grasp of Jennens's text as essentially an audacious experiment on which the pair of them were collaborators.

---

* They are: 'Rejoice greatly, O daughter of Zion', 'He was despised and rejected of men' and 'The trumpet shall sound'.

7

COMPOSING *MESSIAH*

Handel began work on *Messiah* during the summer of 1741, in an intensive three-week burst of creativity that commenced on 27 August and saw a draft score completed on 12 September. He is said to have written part of it while staying at a manor house belonging to Charles Jennens in the Derbyshire village of Snitterton, near Matlock, a spa noted for the treatment of rheumatism, gout and lumbago. Since Handel liked to spend part of each summer in the country and took the waters at Scarborough, Cheltenham and Tunbridge Wells, this idea is not unlikely, though the final section of the work was probably written on his return to London. By 14 September he filled out the score with its recitative passages and instrumentation for a basic orchestra of strings, basso continuo (cello and keyboard) and, in four of the musical items, trumpets and timpani.

The original draft manuscript of *Messiah*, now in the British Library, was taken by Handel to Dublin, where, as we have seen, he made various adaptations and adjustments, adding the names of the singers here and there as an aide-memoire or an indication to the copyist. Along with this went a fair copy, made as a performing score by his friend and principal assistant John Christopher Smith, who had accompanied him to Ireland. Born Johann Christoph Schmidt in Germany in 1683, he had been a fellow student at Halle University with Handel and probably joined him in London around 1717, remaining there for the rest of his life. The presence of a musical copyist was vital in an age when most music still circulated in manuscript rather than printed form. Smith (as he became in England) was an essential collaborator with Handel in the preparation of performing scores and orchestral parts, gathering a team of assistants around him, several of them members of his own family.

Both the autograph and the performing score form the basis of our knowledge of Handel's compositional progress towards a first performance of *Messiah.* Through them we can also follow a trail of successive emendation and recomposition during the work's early presentations to the London audience of the 1740s, a series of needful revisions mostly occasioned by the availability and talents of various different soloists. In addition to these sources there is the score and the set of vocal and instrumental parts made for the Foundling Hospital performances in the 1750s and bequeathed to that institution in Handel's will. These were evidently made under Handel's supervision and feature the oboes and bassoons he had added to the oratorio's orchestration during its early London performances.

An advantage for Handel in setting Jennens's selection of biblical texts was that, unlike an opera or a dramatic oratorio, none of the arias or recitatives belonged to a designated character and the choruses were non-specific in terms of giving voice to a particular echelon or nation. Though here and there among his operas Handel had been able to shuffle this or that number from one protagonist to another, in the interests of enlarging an individual role or accommodating a fresh vocal talent, the aria in a lyric drama remained the basic medium for drawing a strong profile for each character. In *Messiah*, on the other hand, the various arias belong to abstract voices, acting as narrator or commentator, rather than to a king, a queen, a warrior or a princess. The dramatic aspect is still powerfully apparent, as we might expect from Handel, but the drama is universal rather than the domain of a single participant in a fictional or historical narrative.

A more problematic feature lay in the nature of the text itself. Handel had grown used to setting librettos written by poets—Italian, English or German—in which nearly every item is constructed according to a precise metre, whose strong rhythms offer hints as to melodic shape and the structure of musical phrases. During his residence in England, however, he had gained valuable experience of tackling a different kind of text altogether, formed from the Authorized or 'King James' Version of the Holy Bible, the seventeenth-century English rendering of Old Testament Hebrew and New Testament Greek, often making use of translations dating from the Reformation a hundred years earlier. Handel's first encounters with this kind of English prose came during the last years of Queen Anne's reign, when he was commissioned to write a *Te Deum and Jubilate* to celebrate the Treaty of Utrecht, ending the War of the Spanish Succession in 1713. Around the same time he composed his first setting of Psalm 42, 'As pants the hart', as an anthem for the Chapel Royal. This was a text Handel would engage with in five subsequent versions, the most strikingly eloquent of them forming part of a series of anthems written for the Duke of Chandos's private chapel at Cannons Park, north of London.

Handel's authoritative grasp of this Anglican church music form was magnificently revealed in the four anthems written for King George II's coronation in 1727. Each of these is treated with a due sense of its suitability to the different phases of the ceremony, the chordal grandeur of 'Zadok the Priest' making a particular impression, beautifully offset by the leisurely elegance and buoyancy of 'My heart is inditing'. The composer's ultimate mastery of the English anthem as a liturgical form established itself ten years later with the great funeral anthem for Queen Caroline, 'The ways of Zion do mourn', in which the scriptural text carefully collates passages from the Psalms and the books of Samuel, Daniel and Lamentations. This piece in its turn prepared the way for the oratorio *Israel in Egypt* (1739), whose scenario and textual arrangement may have been the work of Charles Jennens. The music of the funeral anthem was utilized here as an opening 'act', transmuted into 'The Lamentations of the Israelites for the Death of Joseph'.

In *Israel in Egypt* Handel was faced for the first time with the challenge of composing a large-scale work making use exclusively of extracts from the Bible. Arranged in three extended episodes—the elegy for Joseph, the visitation of the ten plagues on the Egyptians and the crossing of the Red Sea by the Israelites—the oratorio's dramatic content was shaped almost entirely through the medium of the chorus. The experience of fashioning a piece so markedly different in outline and substance from any of his other oratorios provided a testing ground for Handel where the composition of *Messiah* was concerned. He could prove the merits of what Joseph Addison had recommended twenty years earlier in a *Spectator* essay touching on the subject of English church music and the infinite resources available to composers in setting vernacular sacred texts. As well as 'excellent words', 'a wonderful Variety of them' and 'inspired writing', there was an intrinsic value, according to Addison, in the style and language of the Hebrew scriptures. 'There is a certain

Coldness and Indifference in the Phrases of our European Languages, when they are compared with Oriental Forms of Speech', he observed, 'and it happens very luckily that the Hebrew idioms run into the *English* tongue with a peculiar Grace and Beauty'. English, he maintained, 'has received innumerable Elegancies and Improvements from that infusion of *Hebraism,* which are derived to it out of the Poetical Passages in Holy Writ. They give a Force and Energy to our Expressions, warm and animate our Language, and convey our Thoughts in more ardent and intense Phrases than any that are to be met with in our own Tongue'. Such diction, declared Addison, 'often sets the Mind in a Flame, and makes our Hearts burn within us'.[1]

Handel's heart surely burned within him when he wrote *Messiah.* The story of him having a vision of 'the great God himself'[2] while composing the 'Hallelujah' chorus may be a pious fiction, but his focus on the project was entirely genuine. Such fervent concentration, evident both from the dated sections of the original autograph and from the appearance of the manuscript itself, with its ink blots, smudges, erasures and revisions, was in any case typical of Handel's absorption with the task of creating a new work designed, at this point, for inclusion in a forthcoming London oratorio season. The composer developed individual numbers from sketches, most of which have been lost, though a few ideas remain for the closing 'Amen', the alto air 'He was despised' and the chorus 'Let all the angels of God worship Him'.

Having laid down his musical outline he then added the text and ultimately the instrumental scoring. Inspirations came from the biblical verses themselves, as in 'Rejoice greatly, O daughter of Zion' with its infectious atmosphere of jubilation and festivity, or the sombre restlessness of 'Surely He hath borne our griefs', and also from Handel's razor-sharp awareness of striking effects called for by specific moments in the score. The latter was an aspect of his genius that proved fascinating to masters of a later generation such as Haydn and Beethoven.

Interestingly *Messiah* features few of those borrowings from other composers' works that elsewhere made an essential contribution to Handel's creative process. The fundamental shape of themes and melodies was not something that came easily to him and he often preferred to take a snatch from somebody else's aria or orchestral movement, which he might then be able to transform into something of greater substance and sinew, so that several of his best-known pieces took their flight from another composer's musical invention. 'Let the bright seraphim' in *Samson*, for instance, is based on an aria from Giovanni Porta's opera *Numitore*, while 'Angels ever bright and fair' in *Theodora* derives from a work by Agostino Steffani. Though Porta's *Numitore* gave Handel an idea for the 'Amen' chorus in *Messiah*, most of its other borrowings are from his own compositions, more especially from his chamber duets and trios written to Italian texts. One of these, 'Se tu non lasci amore', underlies

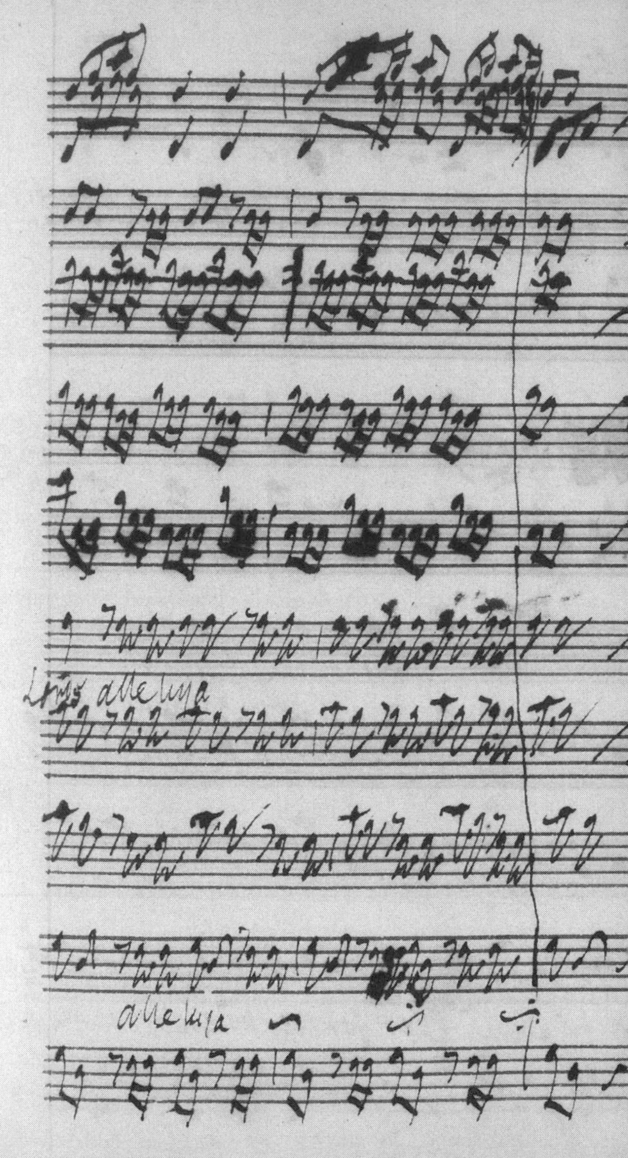
alleluja
alleluja

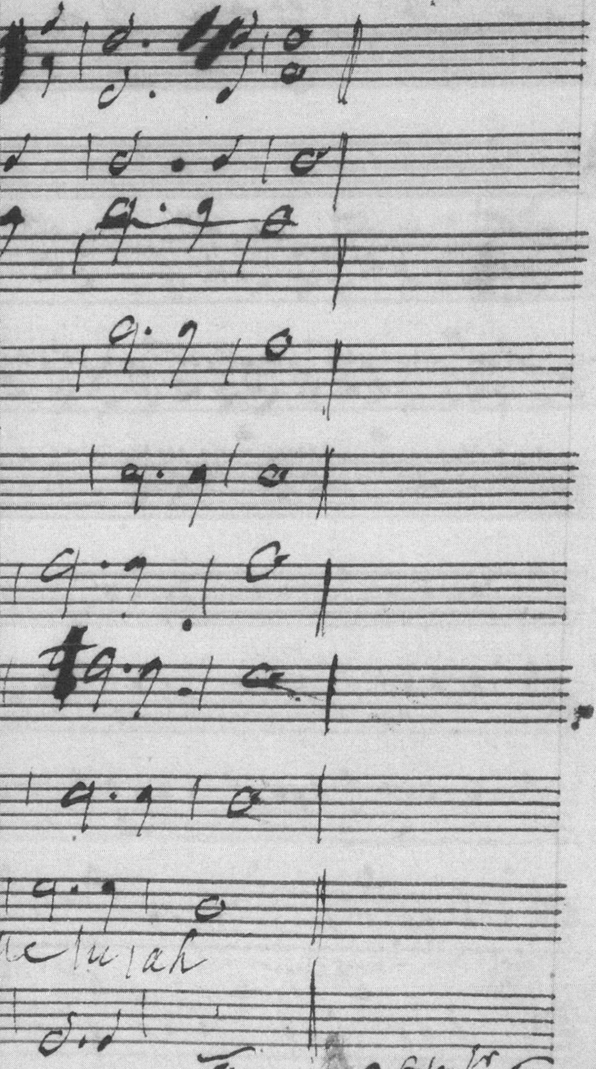

lelujah

☉ Septemb.r 6. 1741.

'O death, where is thy sting?' Two others, 'Quel fior che all'alba ride' and 'No, di voi non vo' fidarmi', were written a few weeks before he began work on the oratorio and their thematic ideas were put to good use in several of the choruses, including 'All we like sheep' and 'For unto us a child is born'.

The phantom presence of these erotic Italian duets in the score of a sacred English-language work exemplifies Handel's sturdy eclecticism. Polyglot, cosmopolitan, always careful never to become entirely absorbed within the culture of that nation in which he had become naturalized, he brought to *Messiah* a freight of worldly experience that, paradoxical as this might seem to some, reinforces rather than diminishes its spirituality. As well as the operatic elements noted earlier, the score, like so much else in Handel's oeuvre, enshrines memories of boyhood training in the churches of his native Halle and of his crucial four-year sojourn in Italy. The 'Hallelujah' chorus, for example, is vitalized with references to the Lutheran chorale 'Wachet auf, ruft uns die

OVERLEAF
The closing bars of the 'Hallelujah chorus', from Handel's draft score of *Messiah*. Handel's taste for striking effects was an aspect of his genius that proved fascinating to masters of a later generation such as Haydn and Beethoven.
CREDIT: © BRITISH LIBRARY BOARD

Stimme' in its setting of 'The kingdom of this world', as also of 'And he shall reign for ever and ever'. Meanwhile the shepherds abiding in the fields take on a specifically Italian guise in the *Pifa*, the pastoral string symphony that introduces them. This and the aria 'He shall feed his flock' make conscious allusions to the music of the *pifferari,* shepherds from the Abruzzi mountains who played their bagpipes in the streets of Rome between Christmas and Epiphany. Such music would have been among the earliest to catch Handel's ear when he arrived in the city in the winter of 1706–7.

Messiah begins, all the same, not in Italy but in France. The opening *Sinfony* is a French overture in the style to which Handel stayed constant, with very few exceptions, throughout his composing career. A slow initial section in dotted rhythm is followed by a fugal allegro. This was a piece Jennens did not care for, but its austerity is a pointer towards the seriousness of intent within the forthcoming musical 'entertainment'. Following what one modern commentator on *Messiah* calls 'the grey cloud-bank of the overture',[3] the shift from its E-minor tonality to the E major of the tenor arioso 'Comfort ye, my people' offers a marked contrast, resonating with that mood of assurance and reassurance that will ultimately prevail in Part III. In the aria that follows, 'Every valley shall be exalted', Handel, sensitive as ever to meaning in his texts, nuances certain words—'the crooked straight and the rough places plain'—through the shape of their musical phrases. The tenor role in *Messiah* might now and then remind us of the Evangelist in the Passion oratorios of the kind Handel would have heard in Germany. He himself wrote one such work, the nowadays unfairly neglected *Brockes Passion*, composed around 1716, and his selection of a tenor voice as the first to be heard in *Messiah* might have been prompted by its traditional association with the Gospel narrator. Yet *Messiah* tells its story via a range of carefully pondered theological implications rather than according to circumstantial events in the life of the Saviour. Thus the tenor takes his place alongside the other soloists in their multiplicity of roles—meditative, prophetic, elegiac and celebratory—together with the chorus as an active participant in the work's successive shifts of mood, pace and discourse.

The changing functional significance devised by Handel for his massed voices is superbly exemplified in Part I. Here the chorus joyfully rounds off the opening sequence with 'And the glory of the Lord', deepens the perspective opened by the alto aria 'But who may abide' and elaborates on the melodic outline of 'O thou that tellest good tidings to Zion'. An edgy chromatic gloom evoked by the bass recitative and aria on the theme of darkness is dispersed for us by the inventive exuberance of 'For unto us a child is born', in whose varied structure we can feel Handel revelling in the rhythmic suppleness of the English text under his musical command. As for the angels' proclamation to the shepherds, the members of the chorus in 'Glory to God' become straightforward actors, materializing and vanishing amid a flurry of strings and trumpets. 'The air vibrates with the pulsation of their innumerable wings',[4] as one delighted Victorian listener puts it. What a modern cliché calls 'accentuating the positive' is the chorus's cheerful assignment in 'His yoke is easy', its buoyancy derived from one of the Italian duets.

Total contrast is ordained for Part II, dwelling as it does on the meaning of Christ's Passion as conveyed to us through the sacrament of the Eucharist. The keys Handel chooses—G minor, E flat, F minor, C minor—are those he associated with inwardness, melancholy and solitude. His use of dotted rhythms in the opening chorus 'Behold the Lamb of God', in the second section of the great alto aria 'He was despised' and in 'Surely He hath borne our griefs' evokes jagged extremes of pain and suffering. A memory of the German Passion oratorio recurs in the scene that follows, where the tenor assumes a narrative voice and the chorus seems to have metamorphosed into the *turba*, the crowd mocking Jesus in 'He trusted in God that He would deliver Him'. This was a chorus to whose character and dramatic role within the oratorio Handel attached major significance. King George III, passionately devoted to his music, wrote that the composer 'was so conscious of the merit of this movement, that he frequently performed it on key'd instruments, as a lesson; and if he was pressed to sit down to play at such times as he felt no immediate impulse, this theme usually presented itself to his mind; when, making it the subject of extemporary fugue and voluntary, it never failed to inspire him with the most sublime ideas and wonderful sallies of imagination'.[5]

Following this, it is up to the tenor to reassure us of Christ's ascension to Heaven in the aria 'But thou didst not leave his soul in hell', a piece whose serene A major underlines the carefully calculated switch of mood. Handel's total command of his resources is conveyed by the emphasis on structural contrasts in 'Lift up your heads, oh ye gates' and 'Let all the angels of God'. The first of these utilizes a double-chorus effect to promote the dialogue content of its text, three verses of Psalm 24, while the second is a densely learned fugue, as appropriate to the angelic choir as is the sheen of its trumpets.

The next episode in the Christian story, making a powerful appeal to Handel's imagination, centres on Whitsun, when the apostles 'spake in tongues', enabling them to preach the Gospel throughout the world. Here the chorus plays the part of Jesus's followers, thrilling us in 'The Lord gave the Word' with a movement that, as one musicologist brilliantly describes it, 'rockets off like an Italian toccata'.[6] The same positively visceral conviction among these disciples is conveyed in 'Their sound is gone out', conceived originally as the second section of 'How beautiful are the feet of them' when the latter began life as a soprano aria. Later 'Their sound is gone out' was transmuted first into a tenor arioso, then into the freestanding choral setting best known today. The bass aria 'Why do the nations so furiously rage together' returns us to the theatre—operatic basses specialized in venting thunderous rage—but the company of missionary apostles from 'Their sound is gone out' bursts in again, when the 'The kings of the earth rise up', wishing to cast off the 'bonds' of religion, their pagan opposition to Christianity is laughed 'to scorn' by 'He dwelleth in Heav'n'. From here it is a short step, via the tenor's exultant 'Thou shalt break them with a rod of iron', whose string figures imitate the ricochet of scornful laughter, to the 'Hallelujah' chorus, that most eagerly awaited moment in every *Messiah* performance. Into somewhat less than four minutes of music Handel compresses an extraordinary diversity of rhythmic tropes, fugal ingenuity and chordal architecture, honouring 'the Lord omnipotent' with resistless assertiveness and exuberance.

This is not quite the end. With the opening of Part III we seem to be a planetary distance away from that glittering affirmation that rounded off the previous act. Another kind of truth is being enunciated for us here, intellectual as well as emotional. Handel took exceptional care, in writing the soprano aria 'I know that my Redeemer liveth', to prevent its transcendent serenity from lapsing into featureless sedateness, conscious as he surely was of the pitfalls created by certain of the monosyllables making up the text. Jennens's attempts at tweaking and tinkering with Handel's setting here did not help, but thankfully the composer's wisdom prevailed and we are left with an air that both rewards the singer and ineffably exalts its hearers.

If Jennens was anxious that listeners should catch the drift of his theological message, then the ensuing chorus 'Since by man came death' drives this home through the eloquent contrast between its slow unaccompanied opening and the faster section, 'By man came also the resurrection'. The proverbial last trumpet of that pivotal moment in Christian experience resonates for us in the bass aria 'The trumpet shall sound', one of the oratorio's few genuine *da capo* arias and a unique opportunity for the soloist to establish a more emphatic presence for himself in the score. After a moment of reflective intimacy, which embraces 'O death, where is thy sting', and the sober beauty of 'If God be for us', the work's choral climax is a magnificent consolidation of a formal device with which Handel had already experimented in *Alexander's Feast*. In that oratorio, a secular piece extolling the power of music, he had added an extra movement, using words by Newburgh Hamilton, to John Dryden's choral finale. In *Messiah* we have in effect three choruses: the monumental 'Worthy is the Lamb', which becomes the grandly contrapuntal 'Blessing and honour and glory and power', before an 'Amen' through whose mighty surges Handel, fusing musical erudition with improvisatory fantasy, set his inimitable stamp on the entire oratorio.

A word needs to be added here as to the instrumentation of *Messiah*. The basic orchestra in Handel's time consisted of a four-part string band—first and second violins, viola (often called a 'tenor' in England) and cello. This last instrument formed part of the basso continuo ensemble, together with a double bass, a harpsichord and the long-necked lute known as a theorbo. The violins could be reinforced with a pair of oboes, while a bassoon was added to the continuo. In Handel's earlier operas the oboes enjoyed solo prominence and he also wrote concertos and sonatas for the instrument. Here and there he enriched this core orchestra with other sounds. Recorders and flutes could be used to highlight the emotional nuances of individual arias, to imitate birdsong or the sound of falling water and to evoke the onset of sleep. Trumpets lent an obvious martial clangour to battle scenes and enhanced the feelings of triumph and jubilation expressed in choral movements, and such moods were also heightened by the use of a pair of horns, first featured by Handel in the *Water Music* and the oratorio *Esther* before being introduced to the opera house in *Radamisto* (1720).

Messiah, during its long performance history, was so frequently reorchestrated (Mozart's 1789 additions for Baron van Swieten in Vienna are an outstanding example) that hearing it played according to Handel's original indications was a fascinating experience for many modern listeners. The oratorio was composed at the end of a phase during which Handel had severely limited the use of oboes in his orchestral palette, so that they hardly feature at all in his last operas, works such as *Serse*, *Imeneo* and *Deidamia.* Thus, initially, the scoring of *Messiah* was limited to the basic Baroque theatre band of strings and continuo, with a soloist added on the eponymous instrument for 'The trumpet shall sound' and further trumpets and timpani in some of the choruses. Those oboes and bassoons whose timbre we are nowadays used to hearing in the choral numbers were introduced by Handel only for his London performances and are not, as far as is known, authentic to the first appearance of the work in Dublin. Yet Alexander Pope's footnote as to Handel's bringing 'more variety of instruments into the Orchestra' and his evocation of those 'hundred hands' shaking and stirring the soul are surely no less valid for being not quite accurate in the case of *Messiah* at the precise moment when the poet paid his fine tribute to the composer.

8

A WORK IN PROGRESS

None of Handel's scores necessarily represents what might be called his last word on the subject. Like other Baroque composers, he saw any composition as being inherently adaptable to circumstance, a work in continual development, open to changes and available to him as a thematic resource or as a piece from which individual segments or numbers could be adapted to other uses. Nowhere is this idea more obvious than in *Messiah*, whose potential during Handel's lifetime for alteration, rewriting or at least recasting is testimony to its toughness and resilience, in both concept and design. The inherent force within Handel's creation, its hold on listeners and performers, derives in significant measure from the oratorio's ability to withstand everything he did to it once the draft score was completed in September 1741. This initial autograph was copied as a performing score for Handel by his secretary and assistant John Christopher Smith, and it was on this score that he based his subsequent changes to different sections of the work.

Once in Ireland Handel would need to alter individual items, sometimes vestigially, sometimes completely overhauling them, according to the particular vocal character and talent of his performers. We should remember that apart from the soprano Cristina Maria Avolio and the violinist and concert-master Matthew Dubourg, he had no idea before setting off on the voyage from Parkgate of the singers and instrumentalists available to him on reaching Dublin. There was work to be done before *Messiah*'s first rehearsals, a process of revision that would also succeed in tightening the oratorio's sinews as a whole and sharpening its effectiveness among those listeners lucky enough to encounter the piece at its very first performance.

A good example of this earliest layer of rewriting is 'But who may abide the day of his coming?', initially cast as an air for bass in a lilting 3/8 before Handel altered it, at this stage, to a recitative, possibly because it had proved too taxing for John Mason, the soloist originally designated from among the singing men, known as lay vicars, of Christ Church and St Patrick's. Perhaps this was also a contributory factor in changes made to 'Why do the nations so furiously rage together', but the result is aesthetically more satisfying in the way the aria's new shape seems to mirror the anarchy and destructiveness evoked by the words, so that the exultant 'Let us break their bonds asunder' gains an additional edge of spontaneity. Further cutting at this stage improved 'Rejoice greatly, O daughter of Zion', somewhat too prolix in its earliest incarnation as a *da capo* aria. For this new version Handel retained the original 12/8 time signature while removing the *da capo* indication and recycled some of the cancelled material to make up a more tautly effective close.

It was for Susanna Cibber that he made two of the most significant revisions to the score before its first performance. The musicologist Charles Burney recalled that 'her voice was a thread and her knowledge of Music very inconsiderable, yet by a natural pathos, and perfect conception of the words, she often penetrated the heart, when others, with infinitely greater voice and skill, could only reach the ear'.[1] This kind of interpretative instinct was a quality Handel seems genuinely to have valued, so that Cibber's presence in the Dublin cast was to be regarded as an asset, whatever her vocal limitations. Thus the beautiful sequence towards the close of Part I that begins with the recitative 'Then shall the eyes of the blind be opened' and leads to the air 'He shall feed his flock' was transposed from soprano in B flat to alto in F. Later in the work a transposition from G minor to C minor allowed Cibber to sing 'If God be for us'. The alto contribution to *Messiah*'s sound world, memorable as it so often proves for listeners, owes much to the happy

Larghetto
But who
and who shall stand
Stand When he
bide but who may a= bide the

= bide the day of his coming
appeareth who shall
But who may a=
his Coming

coincidence that brought the composer and the singing actress together during that momentous Dublin season of 1741–2. As one audience member observed, 'No person of sensibility, who has had the good fortune to hear Mrs Cibber sing in the oratorio of *Messiah*, will find it very difficult to give credit to accounts of the wonderful effects produced from so powerful a union'.[2]

She repeated these 'wonderful effects' when Handel returned to London in August 1742 and applied for a licence to present oratorios at the theatre in Covent Garden, managed by the impresario John Rich. *Messiah* was now scheduled for its first performance in England, to take place in March 1743, after the dramatic oratorio *Samson* had been given its premiere. Once more Handel took his editorial pen in hand. This time, 'Their sound is gone out', which had not featured in the Dublin version, appeared in the guise of a short solo for tenor with continuo accompaniment, and 'But who may abide' was also assigned to the tenor soloist. At this performance the singer was Thomas Lowe, a replacement for the great John Beard, whose talent Handel had nurtured with such success during the past decade and who

OVERLEAF
The aria 'But who may abide the day of his coming', from the Foundling Hospital part-book for Second Soprano.
CREDIT: © THE GERALD COKE HANDEL FOUNDATION, THE FOUNDLING MUSEUM, LONDON

had thrilled the audiences for *Samson* with his interpretation of the title role. Why Beard withdrew at this point from the Covent Garden programme is unknown, yet Handel evidently thought highly enough of Thomas Lowe to create later roles for him, such as Zadok in *Solomon* and Septimius in *Theodora*, each taxing in its technical demands. For his 1743 'But who may abide' Handel's instruction reads, '*Un tono piu alto ex E* for Mr Lowe in tenor cliff'.

During the *Samson* performances that February, Horace Walpole, whose letters offer such a vivid perspective of fashionable London amusement, wrote to a friend, 'Handel has set up an Oratorio against the Operas, and succeeds. He has hired all the goddesses from farces and the singers of *Roast Beef* from between the acts . . . with a man with one note in his voice and a girl without even an one; and so they sing and make brave hallelujahs'.[3] One of the 'goddesses from farces' was Kitty Clive, a captivating Irish actress specializing in comic afterpieces but also scoring a hit as Polly in *The Beggar's Opera*. Handel, who had written a theatre song for her some years earlier, now cleverly chose to cast her as Dalila, Samson's seductress, while also finding a niche for her in *Messiah* by turning the recitative 'But lo, the angel of the Lord' into a full-scale aria.

As we shall see, *Messiah*'s London premiere was not the success either Handel or Charles Jennens might have envisaged, and it was only in the Lenten oratorio season of 1745 that the work was revived for two performances. Jennens

was urging Handel to make crucial adjustments in various areas of the score. Writing to Edward Holdsworth that August, the librettist appears distinctly tepid in evaluating the composer's treatment of his 'collection'. Handel, he says, 'has made a fine Entertainment of it, tho' not near so good as he might & ought to have done. I have with great difficulty made him correct some of the grossest faults in the composition'.[4] If Jennens's strictures resulted in a change of rhythm for 'Rejoice greatly, O daughter of Zion' and a full choral setting of 'Their sound is gone out', then these are both changes for the better. Using common time to replace the earlier dancing measures of the aria gives greater formal contrast to the oratorio's first act. As for the chorus, its new version represents an altogether more dignified and convincing embodiment of the biblical text.

Was Jennens content with this? Perhaps not entirely. His complex character, melancholy and exacting, made him potentially difficult to deal with, but Handel seems to have negotiated their working relationship with consummate skill, and Jennens himself was far too reliant on the emotional solace afforded him by the composer's artistry

The great Handelian tenor John Beard, painted by Thomas Hudson. In *Messiah*'s first London performance, in April 1743, Beard was replaced—for reasons that remain unclear—by Thomas Lowe.
CREDIT: © THE GERALD COKE HANDEL FOUNDATION, THE FOUNDLING MUSEUM, LONDON / BRIDGEMAN IMAGES

to desire an outright quarrel. In 1744, the pair had collaborated on *Belshazzar*, whose text Handel justly praised as 'a Noble Piece, very grand and uncommon',[5] which was given its first performance on 27 March 1745. A failure on this occasion, it is nowadays seen as one of the summits of Handel's art, 'a work of supreme genius whose relevance to our times seems to loom larger with every decade'.[6] Here as elsewhere in the dramatic oratorios of the 1740s, the experience of composing *Messiah*, most of all in the flexibility and expressiveness of the choral medium, had clearly provided its own 'refiner's fire' for Handel's active imagination.

It was not until 1749 that *Messiah* made its first real impact on English audiences. A single performance took place at Covent Garden on 23 March. On this occasion Handel was able to deploy not only an excellent cast of soloists, but larger orchestral forces than usual, so that the contrast of enriched or diminished instrumentation (marked *con ripieno* or *senza ripieno* in the score) added a fresh dimension to the work as received by its audience. Soprano arias and recitatives were divided between an unnamed boy treble, who sang 'How beautiful are the feet of them' and 'If God be for us' in the G minor of the original autograph, and the engaging Italian prima donna Giulia Frasi. Her compatriot Caterina Galli took the alto role; Thomas Lowe reprised most of his tenor numbers and the outstanding bass Henry Reinhold had by now become a regular singer in Handel's oratorio seasons. When Galli died in 1804, an obituary notice would refer to her as 'the last of Mr Handel's scholars'.[7] Much of the breakthrough success of this 1749 *Messiah* was surely due to the fact that all its soloists were to some degree 'Mr Handel's scholars', singers whose special gifts he had singled out and nurtured.

It was another of these pupils, possessor of an exceptional talent, who inspired Handel's last serious retouching of the score. In 1748 the twenty-year-old castrato Gaetano Guadagni had arrived in London, alongside Giulia Frasi, as part of an Italian comic opera troupe. Keen to sing in English as well as in Italian, he went for lessons, at her recommendation, to Charles Burney, who described him as 'very young, wild and idle, with a very fine counter-tenor voice of only six or seven notes compass'.[8] Handel saw obvious potential here, as well as appreciating Guadagni's intelligence and ability to learn quickly, 'idle' though he may have been. When *Messiah* was revived in 1750 the composer returned to 'But who may abide', which had figured as a bass aria at Covent Garden the previous year, and recast it for Guadagni, shortening the second section so that more insistent feeling of pace is carried over from the preceding recitative. The young castrato inspired a further change, this time in 'Thou art gone up on high', which had been given to a bass soloist in the original score before being transferred to a soprano for subsequent performances.

A highly profitable association meanwhile developed between Handel and Gaetano Guadagni. He created the key role of Didymus in *Theodora* and later took part in revivals of ten other oratorios, including *Esther* and *L'Allegro, il Penseroso ed il Moderato*. A brilliant international career during the 1760s witnessed his creation of the title role in Gluck's opera *Orfeo* in Vienna, which he sang on his return to London in 1770. He never forgot Handel's teaching, however, earning criticism in later years for making opera sound too much like oratorio. Showing a copy of the composer's portrait to the Irish tenor Michael Kelly, he described Handel as 'one whom all my life I have made my study and endeavoured to imitate . . . the inspired master of our art'.[9]

Over almost a decade *Messiah* had survived as a work in progress, adapted to the individual requirements or shortcomings of interpreters as diverse as Cibber and Guadagni, subjected to amendment under the influence, well intentioned or purely selfish, of its librettist and revised by a composer for whom initial concepts did not necessarily embody wholly inflexible resolutions. That there is no inviolably 'authentic' version of the oratorio represents one of its most challenging and absorbing features.

9

FINDING AN AUDIENCE

Nowadays *Messiah* occupies an unshakeable position within the core repertoire of large-scale pieces for voices and orchestra. Such a triumph, however, was not immediate. London audiences, awaiting Handel's return from Ireland in August 1742, after ten months' absence, were reluctant at first to give the oratorio the kind of enthusiastic reception they accorded *Samson*, composed at the same time. *Messiah*'s very distinctiveness from what 'the Town' was used to in terms of Handel's English-language choral compositions proved initially disconcerting. In a preface to the printed wordbook for *Samson*, Newburgh Hamilton, as we have seen, praised the composer's introduction of oratorio, describing it as a musical drama with a scriptural subject, whose discourse mingled those of church music and opera. *Messiah*, while it ticks most of these boxes, is not a musical drama of the kind London anticipated. Apart from anything else, it arrived in the English capital without the title carried at its Dublin performances. Handel's Covent Garden subscription concert on 23 March 1743 offered something discreetly labelled 'A New Sacred Oratorio', and when his publisher John Walsh issued a selection of Handel overtures 'fitted to the Harpsicord or Spinnet', this would include the 'Sacred Oratorio' alongside *Saul*, *Deidamia* and the serenata *Il Parnasso in festa*.

Such tentativeness regarding the name perhaps hints at Handel's apprehensions when introducing the new piece to Londoners. His friend Lord Shaftesbury shrewdly noted of this premiere that 'partly from scruples some Persons had entertained against carrying on such a Performance in a Play House and partly for not entering into the genius of the Composition, this Capital Composition was but indifferently relish'd'. One of these dissentient voices belonged to a certain 'Philalethes',* an anonymous contributor to the Tory newspaper the *Universal Spectator* in its issue dated 19 March 1743, four days before the scheduled concert. This 'profess'd Lover of *Musick*', claiming his article to be inspired by 'pious Zeal', with 'nothing derogatory said of Mr *Handel's* merit', first of all laid into the inherent sacrilege of presenting oratorio in a theatre. 'An *Oratorio*', he declared,

* The Greek nom de plume translates as 'lover of truth'.

'either is an *Act* of *Religion*, or it is not; if it is, I ask if the *Playhouse* is a fit *Temple* to perform it in, or a Company of *Players* fit *Ministers* of *God's Word*'.

Deploring this profanation of the Bible, the writer, warming to his theme, squared up directly to the challenge of the new oratorio, dealing with '*God* by the most *sacred*, the most *merciful Name* of *Messiah*; for I'm inform'd that an Oratorio call'd by that Name has already been perform'd in *Ireland*, and is soon to be perform'd *here*'. It was nonsensical, declared Philalethes, to pretend that the experience of listening to an oratorio had a benign devotional influence on people who did not go to church. 'If this Assertion was true, are the most sacred Things, *Religion* and the *Holy Bible* which is the *Word* of *God*, to be prostituted to the perverse Humour of a Set of obstinate People?'[1]

It has been suggested that the indignant Philalethes was a non-juror. If so, perhaps he knew Charles Jennens, who had his own reasons for being unenthusiastic about the oratorio as now presented. 'Messiah was perform'd last night', he reported to Edward Holdsworth, '& will be again tomorrow, notwithstanding the clamour rais'd against it, which has only occasion'd it's being advertis'd without its Name . . . 'Tis after all, in the main, a fine Composition, notwithstanding some weak parts, which he [Handel] was too idle & too obstinate to retouch, tho' I us'd great importunity to perswade him to it'.[2] Jennens was a shade more enthusiastic about the piece as a whole than he had been when

Handel first showed it to him on returning from Ireland. 'His *Messiah* has disappointed me, being set in great haste, tho' he said he would be a year about it, & make it the best of all his Compositions. I shall put no more Sacred Works into his hands, to be thus abus'd'.[3] The whole enterprise, where Jennens was concerned, ought to have represented an ideal collaboration between the composer and his leading enthusiast, from which the crowning masterpiece of Handel's career would emerge after months of painstaking artistry. Instead it had been rushed into existence in a matter of weeks and was now being neglected in favour of *Samson*.

Though there were two further performances of *Messiah* to round off the season, Jennens remained profoundly dissatisfied, less perhaps with its reception than with what he considered Handel's cavalier attitude to the score. Thus when in April 1743 the composer suffered a stroke, presumably another visitation of the 'Paraletick Disorder' that had affected him six years earlier, Jennens was not especially sympathetic. 'I don't yet despair of making him retouch the *Messiah*, at least he shall suffer for his negligence; nay I am inform'd that he has suffer'd, for he told Lord Guernsey that a letter I wrote him about it contributed to the bringing of his last illness upon him'.[4] A sense of unfinished business regarding *Messiah* remained paramount for Jennens, the more so when Handel turned for a new oratorio libretto to William Congreve's erotic drama *Semele*, based on Greek mythology. Jennens later dismissed this as 'a bawdy opera',[5] which from one aspect it might be. In any case the 1744 season of which it formed a part was noteworthy for not including *Messiah*. The two men nevertheless began a new collaboration that summer, on *Belshazzar*, another Jennens text featuring, like *Saul*, undercover non-juror and Jacobite politics wrapped within the respectable integuments of a Bible story. 'I must take him as I find him', concluded the librettist of his composer, 'and make the best use I can of him'.[6]

Messiah returned to the concert platform in 1745, once again at the end of the Lent season, according to what would become Handel's common practice. He always associated it with Easter, rather than with the Christmas or Advent periods during which it is frequently given today. For the first time, no doubt to Jennens's satisfaction, the title was given as *Messiah* and Handel had obliged him with various alterations to the score. The Philalethes tendency, what is more, seems to have remained silent on the subject of religious decorum, Handel being rewarded instead by altogether more sensitive responses to his achievement. An anonymous 'Ode to Mr Handel' actually succeeded in incorporating snatches of the wordbook within its heavily alliterative tribute, at such moments as 'Him, feeder of the flock / And leader of the lambs', 'High Hallelujahs of empyreal hosts' or 'Him pious pity paints / In mournful melody / The man of sorrows'.[7] Maybe the poet had glanced at a similar effusion the previous year by a Mr Delacourt, fresh from hearing 'Mr Handel's grand Oratorio, called the MESSIAH' in St Finbarr's Cathedral at Cork, its first known performance in a church:

Ne'er were my Passions shook, so rouz'd before,
It thrill'd my Blood, my Pulses beat no more;
Death seem'd attentive to th'harmonious Sphere,
And Silence Self sat listening in my Ear.

Delacourt compares himself to one of the shepherds:

Thus Eastern Swains, that kept their Flocks by Night,
Heard Songs Seraphic hymn'd by Sons of Light;
Their Awe-struck Senses seem'd absorb'd and lost,
Drown'd in the Chorus of the Heav'nly Host.[8]

There were to be no more *Messiah* evenings for another four years, until the 1749 concert that commentators see as a major shift in the work's fortunes. By now it had gained acceptance among many of those who might earlier have been tempted to criticize it for possible impiety in its handling of the kind of material that the eighteenth century liked to call 'awful' (i.e., awe-inspiring) and 'solemn'. Added to this critical traction was the interest that attached to the oratorio from purely musical and artistic aspects, especially among the dedicated circle of English patrons, amateurs and enthusiasts, many of them linked to one another by ties of family or friendship, who had gathered around Handel during the 1730s and kept each other informed of his latest works and projects.

The genuine conquest, where *Messiah*'s earliest audiences were concerned, came via Handel's involvement with one of Georgian England's most significant charitable enterprises. In 1739 Captain Thomas Coram, a retired sailor and merchant, succeeded in opening a home for 'exposed and deserted young children' on a site in Bloomsbury. The Foundling Hospital, as it was called, was designed by Theodore Jacobsen, a subscriber to Handel's published scores and one of the orphanage's governors, as was John Walsh, whose firm was the chief diffuser of Handel's music. It might have been Walsh and Jacobsen who invited Handel to a committee meeting on 4 May 1749, when he 'generously and charitably offered a performance of vocal and instrumental musick to be held at this Hospital and that the money arising therefrom should be applied to finishing the chapel of the Hospital'.[9] Once again *Messiah* found itself giving assistance to a charitable undertaking. Just as the Dublin fundraising for Mercer's Hospital and 'the prisoners in the several gaols' had proved auspicious for its very first performance, now Coram's charity set it on course once more, with Handel being offered a governorship of the foundation, a date—27 May—being fixed for the concert and an invitation sent to the Prince and Princess of Wales, both of them Handel enthusiasts. Though the programme for this

occasion was a medley of the composer's vocal and instrumental works, including items from the recently premiered *Solomon* and the *Music for the Royal Fireworks*, Handel managed to fold the 'Hallelujah' chorus into his anthem 'Blessed are they that considereth the poor', made up from his earlier sacred pieces. It also served as an apt introduction of Gaetano Guadagni as soloist to a wider London public.

It was the *Messiah* evening on 1 May 1750 that sealed its connection with the Foundling Hospital during the remaining nine years of Handel's lifetime. He had presented an organ to the chapel, though this was not yet ready for installation. Available in abundance, on the other hand, was an excited audience—rather too much of it as matters turned out, since the building was packed to the doors, many people were turned away and carriages jammed the surrounding streets. A further performance four days later was an equal sell-out, so that the charity made nearly £1,000. Thereafter *Messiah* at the Foundling Hospital became, for a decade at least, an annual London concert fixture.

The details of its presentation there on 15 May 1754 are especially precise, and one of the oratorio's most illuminating modern interpretations, by the conductor and

OVERLEAF
The Foundling Hospital, Bloomsbury. Charitable performances of *Messiah* at the hospital became an annual London concert fixture during the 1750s.
CREDIT: © THE FOUNDLING MUSEUM, LONDON

musicologist Christopher Hogwood, was based on a painstaking reconstruction of the forces then used. Handel's *Messiah* orchestra now included four oboes, four bassoons and two horns, reflecting the increased symphonic instrumental forces of the period. John Beard was once again the tenor soloist and Caterina Galli resumed the alto role briefly taken by Guadagni. The nineteen-strong choir was divided between six Chapel Royal boy trebles and thirteen men singing alto, tenor and bass.

Once again the chapel was packed, though a misunderstanding between Handel and the governors very nearly lost them *Messiah* altogether. For whatever reason the foundation had come to believe that the oratorio was its exclusive property, 'secured' by the composer to the hospital's charitable uses. On this basis the governors moved to obtain confirmation of this through an act of parliament. The composer was having none of that—'the same did not seem agreeable to Mr Handel for the present', noted the minutes—but genuine proof of his good intentions later showed in a codicil to his will, made in 1757, leaving 'a fair copy of the Score and all Parts of my Oratorio called the Messiah to the Foundling Hospital'. The score consists of three volumes and twenty-eight vocal and instrumental parts, all in the hand of professional copyists, made from the 1754 performing material and based on the performing score he had edited and annotated over the twelve years that had elapsed since the Dublin premiere.

The eighteenth-century music historian Sir John Hawkins was the first to note the shift in popular taste that eventually brought about acceptance of a work that undoubtedly took time to find its audience. 'At length a change of sentiment in the public began to manifest itself; the Messiah was received with universal applause'.[10] This was symptomatic of a much wider development in English sensibility, a harbinger of Romanticism to whose awakening impulses Handel's own imagination was responsive. The 1750s were the years in which dramatists in London found a willing audience for what their Parisian counterparts called *comédies larmoyantes*: tear-jerking plays with sentimental happy endings justifying humanity's nobler instincts. The new art of landscape gardening encouraged ideas of nature as a manifestation of the sublime or, for the more spiritually inclined, of God's grandeur on earth. This was an epoch when the thrilling evangelicalism of the Methodists, followers of John Wesley, took hold of religious communities throughout the country, a time when natural catastrophes such as the terrible Lisbon earthquake of 1755 drove hitherto frivolous individuals to take their faith more seriously. People yearned more strongly than before for some apprehension of the lofty, the earnest and the exalted. *Messiah* was an ideal solace and reward for this profound hankering.

10

BLESSING & HONOUR & GLORY & POWER

When Handel died, on 14 April 1759, he was buried in Westminster Abbey, where three years later a monument was raised to him, the work of the French sculptor Louis-François Roubiliac. The latter was well acquainted with the composer, having carved the unique marble image, now in the Victoria and Albert Museum, that had been commissioned originally for installation in Vauxhall Gardens. It shows Handel in his dressing gown and turban-shaped cap, with one slipper off, as a modern Orpheus. Roubiliac had also fashioned a memorable bust of him, a likeness accurate enough to display the mole on his left cheek. The statue is one of the most outstanding achievements in the European sculpture of its period, a pioneering image of a living artist that manages to capture the ideal essence of his music in an almost magical fusion of simplicity, humanity and serene wisdom within a single significant form.

The Westminster Abbey monument has little of the compelling intimacy displayed in either the bust or the Orpheus statue. Handel, robed as a doctor of music, stands rather awkwardly posed against a background of clouds on which rides a seraph playing the harp. Crowded into the right-hand corner of the medieval arch surrounding the ensemble are a pair of musical instruments, a cello and a horn, reminding us of the composer's profession, while on a lectern a score labelled 'MESIAH' [*sic*] lies open. Handel himself, pen in hand, is shown in the act of writing—or having just written—the aria 'I know that my Redeemer liveth'.

This is by no means the happiest of Roubiliac's achievements. The Abbey contains several other more notable examples of his vision and professionalism as an artist, and we can almost feel the sculptor's embarrassment in the process of aiming at, but never quite reaching, the requisite level of sublimity. This Westminster Handel monument has, nevertheless, its own significance in the field of Handelian iconography, as an eloquent demonstration of that worship of

Louis-François Roubiliac's marble statue of Handel as a modern Orpheus was originally commissioned for installation in Vauxhall Gardens.
CREDIT: © CORAM, IN THE CARE OF THE FOUNDLING MUSEUM

the composer that developed in the hundred years following his death, a cult at whose centre *Messiah* had the misfortune to be placed. Surveying the oratorio's destiny during the late eighteenth century and throughout the Victorian era, we are reminded of the comment made on the dead King Lear in Shakespeare's tragedy: 'The wonder is he hath endur'd so much'. The story of *Messiah* is an extraordinary record of artistic survival against fearful odds. It was not just the oratorio itself that suffered at the hands of its admirers, but Handel besides. The fate of certain creative spirits, that their overall achievement is signposted for us by one artefact alone, became—or very nearly became—Handel's own, so that the process of recovering his other works from under *Messiah*'s shadow has been, however ultimately rewarding, a slow one. In the course of that same process, nevertheless, the piece composed in 1741, performed in Dublin in 1742 and given in London in various versions at Covent Garden and the Foundling Hospital, has been convincingly restored to us by musicologists, conductors, singers and instrumentalists. We are somewhat better equipped, as a result, to confront its subtleties and complexities than at any time since 1759.

The same proto-Romantic sensibility we noted earlier as a favouring gale behind the shift in the acceptance of *Messiah* among London audiences encouraged its popularity with choirs and concert societies all over Georgian England. Handel was to be regarded, in the words of one late eighteenth-century provincial enthusiast, as 'pre-eminent, incomparable, transcendent, unrivalled, unequalled'.[1] An ultimate seal on this hagiography came with the grand Westminster Abbey Commemoration festival of 1784, intended to mark the supposed centenary of the composer's birth. Its five concerts, over a three-week period from the end of May to the beginning of June, rallied enormous forces: 257 singers for the chorus and a 250-strong orchestra, which included twenty-six bassoons, twelve trumpets and fifteen double basses. The entire massive ensemble was directed by the amateur musician Joah Bates, whose harpsichord was connected to the organ by a chain mechanism devised originally for Handel himself at Covent Garden. Among the vocal soloists were the German soprano Gertrud Elisabeth Mara, whose fame in London was boosted by her Commemoration performances, and the popular castrato Gasparo Pacchierotti. Heading the audience were King George III and Queen Charlotte, both ardent Handelians in the best traditions of their family. The diarist Silas Neville called the whole affair 'one of the greatest musical performances I ever heard, indeed with regard to the number of bands the greatest. The effect of the first crash of such a band was astonishing. Wonder mixed with pleasure appeared in every countenance. They played in time—excellent time—contrary to all expectations'.[2]

The 1784 Commemoration, it has been rightly observed, gave 'a licence for almost any kind of maltreatment of *Messiah* in the future'.[3] We cannot blame the rising generation in late Georgian England for wanting to honour Handel, but the event, when viewed across two centuries, seems to mark the point at which both the oratorio and its composer start to disappear from view. They became part of a world that had precious little to do with music or artistic impulse, one that was more obviously linked with patriotic ideas of Englishness, Protestantism, collective worship and that inherent democracy of choral singing that played such a vital role in the lives of civic communities in the industrial towns of England's North and Midlands. It was a short step from 1784 to the equally monumental Handel festivities launched at the Crystal Palace in 1857, which from certain aspects marked the nadir of Handel's critical fortunes.

By now what one modern musicologist refers to as 'mythistoria Handeliana',[4] a series of tales and anecdotes surrounding *Messiah* and its composer, had begun to develop. For example, was Handel genuinely favoured by visions of 'the great God himself' when he composed the 'Hallelujah' chorus? And did he honestly tell Lord Kinnoull, who complimented him on 'the noble entertainment which he had lately given the town', 'My Lord, I should be sorry if I only entertained them. I wish to make them better'?[5] And, incidentally, was the custom of standing for the 'Hallelujah' chorus initiated by no less a figure than King George II? Probably not, but by the mid-nineteenth century it had become standard practice and has not altogether died out today.

The Crystal Palace Handel festivals, taking place annually until after the Great War, might be viewed as a celebration of Victorian England's impulse towards feeling good about itself. What was later termed 'the great Handelian solemnity'[6] became a vehicle for a certain degree of moral smugness and self-satisfaction, deriving from an image of the composer entirely at odds with the figure we now know—or think we know—from subsequent musicological research. 'As to the good arising from the Handel Festival', wrote a reviewer in 1880, 'there can be no doubt. It displays, and also confirms, the public allegiance to a master absolutely blameless in the character and tendency of his works'.[7] Those works, meanwhile, had been substantially reorchestrated, with the addition of instruments alien to their original scores or unknown in Handel's time, so as to be sufficiently audible in Joseph Paxton's glass-and-cast-iron exhibition hall, moved to Sydenham from its original site in Kensington Gardens.

As with the 1784 Commemoration, nothing at the Crystal Palace was spared as regards the sheer scale and immensity of the choral and orchestral forces involved. The Handel evoked on these occasions was not the composer as we recognize him from his works or from the reminiscences of his friends and contemporaries. For the Victorians this adoptive Englishman had become a totem of national respectability, the object of a species of uncritical worship that could do nothing but harm to his reputation as a composer. On this

ESTHER
SAMSON
MESSIAH

SAUL
JUDAS
DEBORAH

nineteenth-century high tide of Handelmania *Messiah* rode secure, establishing itself at the centre of the repertoire of choral societies across Great Britain, while enjoying a similar status in the United States. Though the oratorio is not a specifically Protestant work in terms of religious content, it became acceptable, on the basis of a biblical libretto, to the robust evangelicalism of chapel-going Baptists, Methodists and Mormons, its performance, either partial or complete, forming a key element in the devotional year for almost every Protestant denomination on either side of the Atlantic. What is more, in northern English cities such as Leeds and Manchester, the inclusion of *Messiah* in the concert repertoire of local orchestras and festivals drew a significant audience from among the local Jewish community.

What did those listening to Handel in the Crystal Palace, the Free Trade Hall or the chapels and auditoriums of New York, Boston and Chicago actually hear that was authentic to the piece as originally conceived by its creator? A comment by the American essayist Ralph Waldo Emerson is worth noting. Following a *Messiah* performance on

OVERLEAF
'Big-band' Handel: the Crystal Palace Handel festivals were launched in 1857. Not until the arrival of the period-instrument movement of the second half of the twentieth century would *Messiah* be restored to its original colours.
CREDIT: © THE GERALD COKE HANDEL FOUNDATION, THE FOUNDLING MUSEUM, LONDON

Christmas Day 1843, he recalled, 'I walked in the bright paths of sound, and liked it best when the long continuance of a chorus had made the ear insensible to music, made it as if there was none; then I was quite solitary and at ease in the melodious uproar'.[8] The impression here is of the score as a kind of monstrous, all-pervasive blur, its details buried beneath the era's growing obsession with abundance and profusion in everything from the façade of a museum or a railway station to the various courses of a dinner menu. What seems to be happening, at least in Emerson's imagination, is that *Messiah* is being transformed into a species of meta-music, annihilating its own artistic identity under the suffocating weight of the various forms of enthusiasm evinced by its performers and those who listen to them. The result appears ominous for both the oratorio and its composer and so indeed it was to prove.

Thus the grandeur of proportion typifying a Crystal Palace choir and orchestra as it prepared to launch itself on *Messiah* was dictated not simply by the size and resonance of Paxton's exhibition hall re-erected in south London, but quite as much by what the audience believed was appropriate to the character of the oratorio and its composer. The whole issue of additional orchestration, while seen as essential under such circumstances, nevertheless troubled several of the more musically scrupulous visitors to the annual festival. The target of their criticism was the Neapolitan conductor Michael Costa, a naturalized Briton who had become a dominant figure on the London musical scene. Presiding over the Crystal Palace oratorio concerts in their early years and directing a massed choir of nearly three thousand voices and a band of 460 musicians, he had no scruples about re-composing Handel when it suited. Sir George Grove, author of the musical encyclopedia that, as *The Grove Dictionary*, remains an ongoing reference resource project, was outraged by Costa's additions and interpolations: 'They were shameful; it is the only word! So vulgar, so unnecessary, so out of keeping!'[9] Grove particularly disliked the incessant use of 'the "big drum"—enormous, it should be called, for it was the biggest ever made', whose brutal monotony merely furnished further proof, as far as he was concerned, of Costa's ignorance and insensitivity.

It was this drowning of *Messiah* beneath a Victorian obsession with immensity of scale and lavishness of resources that provoked one of the most powerful of all protests from a contemporary listener. In 1891 George Bernard Shaw, not yet a successful dramatist but already an exceptionally witty and perceptive music critic, wrote an article deploring 'the impossibility of obtaining justice for *Messiah* in a Christian country', urging that 'the perfect church-going mood' of Handel performances be replaced by 'a mood of active intelligence' and bewailing a situation in which 'we get broken in to the custom of singing Handel as if he meant nothing'. According to Shaw, 'we know rather less about him than they do in the Andaman Islands, since the Andamans are only unconscious of him, whereas we are misconscious'. His proposal was that 'instead of wasting huge sums on the multitudinous dullness of a Handel Festival', someone should mount 'a thoroughly rehearsed and exhaustively studied performance . . . with a chorus of twenty capable artists. Most of us would be glad to hear the work seriously performed before we die'.[10]

Not long after Shaw wrote his diatribe—and perhaps to some degree inspired by it—a movement began towards restoring *Messiah* to its just proportions, vocal and instrumental. At Cambridge in 1894 the musicologist A. H. Mann mounted the first version of the oratorio to acknowledge a distinction between the performing styles of Handel's day and those of the current epoch, basing its musical text on sedulous research among the original manuscript sources. As Donald Burrows remarks in a modern monograph on *Messiah*, 'Mann, in combining scholarship with a practical intent . . . may be regarded as the father of modern *Messiah* studies'.[11]

Regrettably this scrupulousness was not of a kind that, as yet, recommended itself to contemporary conductors, orchestras or singers. The edition of the oratorio prepared by Ebenezer Prout for inclusion in Novello's series of vocal scores and published in 1904 remained in use for at least another half-century, but its approach to the musical text and the different revisions and rewritings made by Handel himself for early performances was workmanlike rather than scholarly. Sir Thomas Beecham's comments in an essay accompanying a *Messiah* recording issued in 1959 show how robust was the survival, beyond the Victorian era, of an approach to Handel as a kind of musical invalid, requiring plenty of extra vitamins and dietary supplements if his achievement was to endure. 'Sixty years' study of his life and works', claimed the ebullient old maestro, 'have led me to think that he would have raised little objection to some modernization of the instrumental portion of his oratorios'. Beecham went on to advance the classically disingenuous 'Handel would have approved' argument that can still now and then be heard from those inclined to embellish and elaborate on the composer's scores with the help of a whole range of anachronistic musical effects and resources. 'Without some effort along these lines', he declared, 'the greater portion of [Handel's] magnificent output will remain unplayed, possibly to the satisfaction of drowsy armchair purists, but hardly to the advantage of the keenly alive and enquiring concertgoer'.[12]

Beecham was only mildly aware of a gathering interest in what, as something loosely labelled 'early music', had hitherto been widely considered as a domain frequented solely by musicologists, palaeographers and researchers into period instruments. By 1959, however, his *Messiah* recording was itself already something of a quaint anachronism. Nine years previously the case for a performance using the forces envisaged by George Bernard Shaw was eloquently made by John

Tobin and the London Choral Society at a concert in St Paul's Cathedral. Despite the building's notoriously unaccommodating acoustic, the evening was a revelation in demonstrating just how wrong, even before Sir Thomas Beecham had articulated it, was the view that Handel might not survive unless his scores were given a seriously modern makeover. Tobin's *Messiah* was praised for being 'cleaned like the pictures in the National Gallery and with equally startling results'.[13] The way was now clear for fresh approaches to the work, mirrored in an extensive scrutiny of the manuscript sources, which bore fruit in new performing editions by Tobin himself (1965), Watkins Shaw (1959) and Donald Burrows (1987).

An astonishing shift in Handel's fortunes during the past fifty years has rescued the composer's prolific oeuvre, especially the operas, from the utter neglect into which most of it fell during the two centuries that had elapsed since his death in 1759. Musicological research since the mid-twentieth century has uncovered a wealth of detail regarding the man himself, and scholarship has brought us exemplary modern editions of his works in their entirety. The interest in establishing adequate performing techniques for the music of the Baroque, the technology of instrument-making and the training of singers in a vocal style to carry the musical phrases and paragraphs of the Handelian idiom in aria and recitative have all of them been matched by the receptivity and enthusiasm of contemporary audiences, responsive to a voice that resonates the more powerfully without the dubious benefits of interference à la Beecham, let alone of Michael Costa and his big drum. At the oratorio performances featured by modern festivals dedicated to the composer, such as those in Göttingen, Halle and London, the dubious amalgam of nationalism and religious piety that drew the Victorians to Crystal Palace is no longer a necessary validation of Handel's genius. Shorn of its orchestral accretions and performed with something like that ideal 'chorus of twenty capable artists' desired by Shaw, *Messiah* has long shed its status as a national religious totem and re-emerged as a valid work of art, its indwelling subtlety, grace and sinew experiencing their own form of resurrection and redemption. With a more widespread knowledge of Baroque musicians and their world now available to us, whether as listeners or as performers, we are able to see the oratorio in its broader relationship to Handel's output, whether in this or other musical genres, and to the sensitivities, ideals and aspirations of the age in which he lived.

As *Messiah* has taken its proper place within the overall scheme of this remarkable Handelian renaissance, attention has focused inevitably on the issue of what is loosely referred to as the composer's spirituality. There is not the slightest evidence that Handel ever swerved from the Protestant Christianity in which he had been brought up. His forebears, who included Lutheran pastors, were noted as having suffered during the Thirty Years War for their adherence to 'the pure evangelical truth', and he remained constant to the beliefs his family had instilled within him. While in Italy he composed music for the Catholic liturgy—the stupendous setting of *Dixit Dominus* offers a notable example—but he is known to have resisted efforts by cardinals and others to bring him over to the Roman Church. As a resident in London he worshipped at St George's, Hanover Square, where he had his own pew in the church. He wrote three hymn tunes for Charles Wesley, one of the founders of Methodism, and was visited on his deathbed by two leading members of the sect: Selina, Lady Huntingdon; and Colonel Martin Madan. He nevertheless died as he had lived, a Lutheran communicant within the Church of England. In short, he was anything but a 'good old pagan at heart',[14] as one nineteenth-century writer sought to label him.

Modern writers on Handel have tended to make too glib a distinction, however, between his own approach to the treatment of spiritual issues in music and that of his admired musical contemporary, Johann Sebastian Bach. The received view is that the latter, in works such as the Mass in B minor and the two settings of the Passion story, touches depths of spiritual understanding to which Handel either could not reach or never actually wished to. Yet a comparison in this respect between two composers so different in character and style, let alone in the way each chose to direct his gifts, seems otiose and unserviceable to both.

Messiah has nevertheless suffered from this tendency to pigeonhole Handel as a cynical opportunist, a shrewd entertainer with an eye on the market, and Bach as a species of visionary hermit, communing with God through the medium of staves, clefs and semiquavers. The matter is not so simple. *Messiah* might have suffered, over almost 300 years, from its own popularity, yet it is this very same sense of worldly immediacy that invites us to accept another kind of spiritual experience altogether—one that acknowledges the worth of our essential humanity, however flawed and imperfect it may be; one in which, to use the words of an English poet, 'We feel that we are greater than we know'. Sincere and practising Christians both, George Frideric Handel and Charles Jennens created *Messiah* for a Christian audience, yet it consistently manages to transcend the limits of religious and confessional dogma. Its emotional range, the ways in which it embraces the multiplicity of existence, the directness of its engagement with our longing, our fears, our sorrows, our ecstasy and exaltation, give the whole achievement an incomparable universality. *Messiah* knows who we are and speaks to us all.

The seventy-one-year-old Handel in 1756, in a painting by Thomas Hudson. On a table next to the composer is a copy of *Messiah*. The composer who stares calmly out of the portrait had, in fact, been almost entirely blind since 1752.
CREDIT: © PHOTO RESEARCHERS, INC / ALAMY STOCK PHOTO

APPENDIX I

Libretto of *Messiah*

MESSIAH
A SACRED ORATORIO
Words by Charles Jennens
PART I

1 *Sinfonia* (Overture)

2 Accompagnato *Tenor*

Comfort ye, comfort ye my people, saith your God. Speak ye comfortably to Jerusalem, and cry unto her, that her warfare is accomplished, that her iniquity is pardoned. The voice of him that crieth in the wilderness; prepare ye the way of the Lord; make straight in the desert a highway for our God.
(Isaiah 40:1–3)

3 Air *Tenor*

Ev'ry valley shall be exalted, and ev'ry mountain and hill made low; the crooked straight and the rough places plain.
(Isaiah 40:4)

4 Chorus

And the glory of the Lord shall be revealed, and all flesh shall see it together: for the mouth of the Lord hath spoken it.
(Isaiah 40:5)

5 Accompagnato *Bass*

Thus saith the Lord, the Lord of hosts: Yet once a little while and I will shake the heavens and the earth, the sea and the dry land. And I will shake all nations; and the desire of all nations shall come. The Lord, whom ye seek, shall suddenly come to His temple, even the messenger of the Covenant, whom you delight in; behold, He shall come, saith the Lord of hosts.
(Haggai 2:6–7; Malachi 3:1)

6 Air *Alto or soprano*

But who may abide the day of His coming, and who shall stand when He appeareth? For He is like a refiner's fire.
(Malachi 3:2)

7 Chorus

And He shall purify the sons of Levi, that they may offer unto the Lord an offering in righteousness.
(Malachi 3:3)

8 Recitative *Alto*

Behold, a virgin shall conceive and bear a son, and shall call His name Emmanuel, God with us.
(Isaiah 7:14; Matthew 1:23)

9 Air *Alto*

O thou that tellest good tidings to Zion, get thee up into the high mountain. O thou that tellest good tidings to Jerusalem, lift up thy voice with strength; lift it up, be not afraid; say unto the cities of Judah, behold your god! Arise, shine, for thy light is come, and the glory of the Lord is risen upon thee.

Chorus
O thou that tellest . . .
(Isaiah 40:9; 60:1)

10 Accompagnato *Bass*

For behold, darkness shall cover the earth, and gross darkness the people; but the Lord shall arise upon thee, and His glory shall be seen upon thee. And the Gentiles shall come to thy light, and kings to the brightness of thy rising.
(Isaiah 60:2–3)

11 Air *Bass*

The people that walked in darkness have seen a great light; and they that dwell in the land of the shadow of death, upon them hath the light shined.
(Isaiah 9:2)

12 Chorus

For unto us a child is born, unto us a son is given, and the government shall be upon His shoulder; and His name shall be called Wonderful, Counsellor, the mighty God, the Everlasting Father, the Prince of Peace.
(Isaiah 9:6)

13 *Pifa* ('Pastoral Symphony')

14a Recitative *Soprano*

There were shepherds abiding in the field, keeping watch over their flocks by night.
(Luke 2:8)

14b Accompagnato *Soprano*

And lo, the angel of the Lord came upon them, and the glory of the Lord shone round about them, and they were sore afraid.
(Luke 2:9)

15 Recitative *Soprano*

And the angel said unto them: 'Fear not, for behold, I bring you good tidings of great joy, which shall be to all people. For unto you is born this day in the city of David a Saviour, which is Christ the Lord'.
(Luke 2:10–11)

16 Accompagnato *Soprano*

And suddenly there was with the angel, a multitude of the heavenly host, praising God, and saying:
(Luke 2:13)

17 Chorus

'Glory to God in the highest, and peace on earth, good will towards men'.

(Luke 2:14)

18 Air *Soprano*

Rejoice greatly, O daughter of Zion; shout, O daughter of Jerusalem! Behold, thy King cometh unto thee; He is the righteous Saviour, and He shall speak peace unto the heathen. Rejoice greatly . . . [*da capo*]

(Zechariah 9:9–10)

19 Recitative *Alto*

Then shall the eyes of the blind be opened, and the ears of the deaf unstopped. Then shall the lame man leap as an hart, and the tongue of the dumb shall sing.

(Isaiah 35:5–6)

20 Air (or Duet) *(Alto &) soprano*

He shall feed His flock like a shepherd; and He shall gather the lambs with His arm, and carry them in His bosom, and gently lead those that are with young. Come unto Him, all ye that labour, come unto Him that are heavy laden, and He will give you rest. Take his yoke upon you, and learn of Him, for He is meek and lowly of heart, and ye shall find rest unto your souls.

(Isaiah 40:11; Matthew 11:28–9)

21 Chorus

His yoke is easy, and His burden is light.

(Matthew 11:30)

PART II

22 Chorus

Behold the Lamb of God, that taketh away the sin of the world.
(John 1:29)

23 Air *Alto*

He was despised and rejected of men, a man of sorrows and acquainted with grief. He gave His back to the smiters, and His cheeks to them that plucked off His hair: He hid not His face from shame and spitting.
He was despised . . . [*da capo*]
(Isaiah 53:3; 53:6)

24 Chorus

Surely He hath borne our griefs, and carried our sorrows! He was wounded for our transgressions, He was bruised for our iniquities; the chastisement of our peace was upon Him.
(Isaiah 53:4–5)

25 Chorus

And with His stripes we are healed.
(Isaiah 53:5)

26 Chorus

All we like sheep have gone astray; we have turned every one to his own way. And the Lord hath laid on Him the iniquity of us all.
(Isaiah 53:6)

27 Accompagnato *Tenor*

All they that see Him laugh Him to scorn; they shoot out their lips, and shake their heads, saying:

(Psalm 22:7)

28 Chorus

'He trusted in God that He would deliver Him; let Him deliver Him, if He delight in Him'.

(Psalm 22:8)

29 Accompagnato *Tenor*

Thy rebuke hath broken His heart: He is full of heaviness. He looked for some to have pity on Him, but there was no man, neither found He any to comfort him.

(Psalm 69:20)

30 Arioso *Tenor*

Behold, and see if there be any sorrow like unto His sorrow.

(Lamentations 1:12)

31 Accompagnato *Soprano or tenor*

He was cut off out of the land of the living: for the transgressions of Thy people was He stricken.

(Isaiah 53:8)

32 Air *Soprano or tenor*

But Thou didst not leave His soul in hell; nor didst Thou suffer Thy Holy One to see corruption.

(Psalm 16:10)

33 Chorus

Lift up your heads, O ye gates; and be ye lift up, ye everlasting doors; and the King of Glory shall come in. Who is this King of Glory? The Lord strong and mighty, The Lord mighty in battle. Lift up your heads, O ye gates; and be ye lift up, ye everlasting doors; and the King of Glory shall come in. Who is this King of Glory? The Lord of Hosts, He is the King of Glory.
(Psalm 24:7–10)

34 Recitative *Tenor*

Unto which of the angels said He at any time: 'Thou art My Son, this day have I begotten Thee?'
(Hebrews 1:5)

35 Chorus

Let all the angels of God worship Him.
(Hebrews 1:6)

36 Air *Alto or soprano*

Thou art gone up on high; Thou hast led captivity captive, and received gifts for men; yea, even from Thine enemies, that the Lord God might dwell among them.
(Psalm 68:18)

37 Chorus

The Lord gave the word; great was the company of the preachers.
(Psalm 68:11)

38 Air (or Duet and Chorus) *Soprano or alto (or soprano, alto and chorus)*

How beautiful are the feet of them that preach the gospel of peace, and bring glad tidings of good things.
(Isaiah 52:7; Romans 10:15)

39 Chorus (or Air for tenor)

Their sound is gone out into all lands, and their words unto the ends of the world.
(Romans 10:18; Psalm 19:4)

40 Air (or Air and Recitative) *Bass*

Why do the nations so furiously rage together, and why do the people imagine a vain thing? The kings of the earth rise up, and the rulers take counsel together against the Lord, and against His anointed.
(Psalm 2:1–2)

41 Chorus

Let us break their bonds asunder, and cast away their yokes from us.
(Psalm 2:3)

42 Recitative *Tenor*

He that dwelleth in Heav'n shall laugh them to scorn; The Lord shall have them in derision.
(Psalm 2:4)

43 Air *Tenor*

Thou shalt break them with a rod of iron; thou shalt dash them in pieces like a potter's vessel.

(Psalm 2:9)

44 Chorus

Hallelujah: for the Lord God Omnipotent reigneth. The kingdom of this world is become the kingdom of our Lord, and of His Christ; and He shall reign for ever and ever. King of Kings, and Lord of Lords. Hallelujah!

(Revelation 19:6; 11:15; 19:16)

PART III

45 Air *Soprano*

I know that my Redeemer liveth, and that He shall stand at the latter day upon the earth. And though worms destroy this body, yet in my flesh shall I see God. For now is Christ risen from the dead, the first fruits of them that sleep.

(Job 19:25–6; I Corinthians 15:20)

46 Chorus

Since by man came death, by man came also the resurrection of the dead. For as in Adam all die, even so in Christ shall all be made alive.

(I Corinthians 15:21–2)

47 Accompagnato *Bass*

Behold, I tell you a mystery; we shall not all sleep, but we shall all be changed in a moment, in the twinkling of an eye, at the last trumpet.

(I Corinthians 15:51–2)

48 Air *Bass*

The trumpet shall sound, and the dead shall be raised incorruptible, and we shall be changed. For this corruptible must put on incorruption and this mortal must put on immortality. The trumpet . . . [*da capo*]

(I Corinthians 15:52–3)

49 Recitative *Alto*

Then shall be brought to pass the saying that is written: 'Death is swallowed up in victory'.

(I Corinthians 15:54)

50 Duet *Alto and tenor*

O death, where is thy sting? O grave, where is thy victory? The sting of death is sin, and the strength of sin is the law.

(I Corinthians 15: 55–6)

51 Chorus

But thanks be to God, who giveth us the victory through our Lord Jesus Christ.

(I Corinthians 15:57)

52 Air *Soprano and alto*

If God be for us, who can be against us? Who shall lay anything to the charge of God's elect? It is God that justifieth, who is he that condemneth? It is Christ that died, yea rather, that is risen again, who is at the right hand of God, who makes intercession for us.
(Romans 8:31; 8:33–4)

53 Chorus

Worthy is the Lamb that was slain, and hath redeemed us to God by His blood, to receive power, and riches, and wisdom, and strength, and honour, and glory, and blessing. Blessing and honour, glory and power, be unto Him that sitteth upon the throne, and unto the Lamb, for ever and ever. Amen.
(Revelation 5:12–14)

APPENDIX II

Jennens's Scenic Structure for *Messiah*

PART I

'The prophecy and realisation of God's plan to redeem mankind by the coming of the Messiah'

Scene 1:

'Isaiah's prophecy of salvation' (movements 2–4)

Scene 2:

'The prophecy of the coming of Messiah and the question, despite (1), of what this may portend for the World' (movements 5–7)

Scene 3:

'The prophecy of the Virgin Birth' (movements 8–12)

Scene 4:

'The appearance of the Angels to the Shepherds' (movements 13–17)

Scene 5:

'Christ's redemptive miracles on earth' (movements 18–21)

PART II

'The accomplishment of redemption by the sacrifice of Christ, mankind's rejection of God's offer, and mankind's utter defeat when trying to oppose the power of the Almighty'

Scene 1:

'The redemptive sacrifice, the scourging and the agony on the cross' (movements 22–30)

Scene 2:

'His sacrificial death, His passage through Hell and Resurrection' (movements 31–2)

Scene 3:

'His ascension' (movement 33)

Scene 4:

'God discloses his identity in Heaven' (movements 34–5)

Scene 5:

'Whitsun, the gift of tongues, the beginning of evangelism' (movements 36–9)

Scene 6:

'The world and its rulers reject the Gospel' (movements 40–41)

Scene 7:

'God's triumph' (movements 42–4)

PART III

'A Hymn of Thanksgiving for the final overthrow of Death'

Scene 1:

'The promise of bodily resurrection and redemption from Adam's fall' (movements 45–6)

Scene 2:

'The Day of Judgement and general Resurrection' (movements 47–8)

Scene 3:

'The victory over death and sin' (movements 49–52)

Scene 4:

'The glorification of the Messianic victim' (movement 53)

APPENDIX III

Timeline of the Life and Times of George Frideric Handel

1685	23 February: Georg Friedrich Händel born in Halle, Saxony, second son of Dr Georg Händel and his second wife Dorothea Taust.
1692	Handel receives composition lessons from Friedrich Wilhelm Zachow, organist of Halle's Liebfrauenkirche.
1702	Handel attends Halle University as a law student.
1703	Leaves Halle for Hamburg, where he joins the opera house orchestra as a violinist and keyboard player.
1705	His first opera, *Almira*, is produced in Hamburg.
1706	Travels to Italy, probably visiting Venice and Florence before arriving in Rome.

1707 Composes his first oratorio, *Il trionfo del tempo e del disinganno*, and Latin vesper psalms, including *Dixit Dominus.*

1708 Probably visits Florence, where his opera *Vincer se stesso e la maggior vittoria* (*Rodrigo*) is produced; returns to Rome, thence to Naples, where he composes the serenata *Aci, Galatea e Polifemo.*

1709 His opera *Agrippina* is performed at Venice's San Giovanni Grisostomo theatre; Handel returns to Germany, where he is appointed *Kapellmeister* to Georg Ludwig, Elector of Hanover; makes his first visit to London.

1711 His opera *Rinaldo* is performed at the Queen's Theatre, Haymarket.

1713 Composes the *Utrecht Te Deum and Jubilate* and is granted an annual pension of £200.

1714 Queen Anne dies and is succeeded by Elector Georg Ludwig as King George I.

1717 Handel writes the *Water Music* to accompany a royal river trip; he begins composing anthems for the Duke of Chandos.

1718 Composes *Acis and Galatea*, a pastoral serenata, and *Esther*, a sacred drama, for the Duke of Chandos.

1719 The Royal Academy of Music, a scheme for subscription opera seasons at the King's Theatre, Haymarket, is established, with Handel as musical director; he leaves for Germany to engage Italian singers in Dresden.

1723 Appointed composer to the Chapel Royal, for which he receives a second pension of £200; moves to the house in Brook Street where he will spend the rest of his life; appointed music master to royal princesses, with third pension of £200.

1724 Composes the opera *Tamerlano;* premiere of opera *Giulio Cesare.*

1725 Composes the opera *Rodelinda.*

1727 Handel becomes a naturalized British citizen; King George I dies and is succeeded by his son as George II, at whose coronation four new anthems by Handel are performed.

1728 The Royal Academy of Music presents its last season at the King's Theatre.

1729 Handel is contracted by the impresario John Jacob Heidegger to present operas at the King's Theatre.

1732 Composes a revised version of *Esther* for concert performance at the King's Theatre.

1733 A rival opera initiative, later referred to as the 'Opera of the Nobility', begins in London; Handel visits Oxford, where he presents his oratorio *Athalia.*

1734 The opera *Ariodante* is performed at the new theatre in Covent Garden.

1735 The opera *Alcina* is performed at Covent Garden.

1736 Handel composes *Alexander's Feast*, 'an ode set to musick'.

1737 After suffering a severe stroke, Handel takes a cure at the baths of Aachen, Germany; Queen Caroline, wife of George II, dies; Handel composes her funeral elegy, 'The ways of Zion do mourn'.

1738 Composes the oratorios *Saul* and *Israel in Egypt.*

1739 September: Handel writes his 'Twelve Grand Concertos' for string orchestra, published as Op. 6.

1740 Composes *L'Allegro, il Penseroso ed il Moderato.*

1741 Handel's last opera, *Deidamia*, is performed at Lincoln's Inn Fields theatre; 22 August–14 September: composes *Messiah*; leaves for Ireland; 18 November: arrives in Dublin; 23 December: first concert season at the New Music Hall, Fishamble Street, opens.

1742 13 April: *Messiah* receives its premiere at the New Music Hall, Fishamble Street; Handel returns to London.

1743 23 March: first London performance of *Messiah*, as part of Handel's Covent Garden oratorio season.

1744 Handel composes *Hercules*, a 'musical drama', and *Belshazzar*, an oratorio.

1745 Charles Edward Stuart, 'the Young Pretender', heir to the exiled Stuart claimant to the British throne, raises a rebellion in Scotland.

1746 Handel presents *The Occasional Oratorio* as a response to the rebellion; the Pretender's army is defeated at Culloden.

1749 Writes the *Music for the Royal Fireworks*, performed in London's Green Park as part of a celebration of the Peace of Aix-la-Chapelle, ending the War of the Austrian Succession.

1750 The oratorio *Theodora* receives its premiere at Covent Garden; 1 May: *Messiah* first performed at the Foundling Hospital.

1751 Handel completes *Jephtha*, his last oratorio, despite the onset of partial blindness.

1753 The composer is reported to be suffering from total blindness but continues to conduct oratorios, to play the organ and to compose with the help of an amanuensis.

1759 14 April: Handel dies at his house in Brook Street; 20 April: is buried in Westminster Abbey, with three thousand people attending the funeral.

NOTES

CHAPTER 1 A COMPOSER AT THE CROSSROADS

1 London *Evening Post*, 13 May 1737.
2 London *Daily Post*, 4 April 1741.

CHAPTER 2 THE WORLD OF ORATORIO

1 Lord Percival, quoted in Jonathan Keates, *Handel: The Man and His Music*, 2nd edn (London, 2008), p. 187.
2 *Faulkner's Dublin Journal*, 19 April 1732.

CHAPTER 3 TO THE HIBERNIAN SHORE

1 *Faulkner's Dublin Journal*, 24 December 1741.
2 Anon, quoted in Richard Luckett, *Handel's* Messiah: *A Celebration* (London, 1992), p. 64.
3 *Faulkner's Dublin Journal*, 19 November 1741.

4 Morris R. Brownell, 'Ears of an Untoward Make: Pope and Handel', *Musical Quarterly* 62 (1978), (pp. 554–70).

5 Ibid.

6 Alexander Pope, *The Dunciad*, Book IV, in *The Works of Alexander Pope*, vol. III (London, 1770), p. 195.

7 *The Dunciad*, Book IV, ll. 63–70.

8 Laetitia Pilkington, *Memoirs*, 1754, quoted in Keates, *Handel*, p. 286.

9 *Faulkner's Dublin Journal*, 24 November 1741.

CHAPTER 4 ELEVATED, MAJESTIC AND MOVING

1 Handel to Charles Jennens, 29 December 1741, in Eric H. Muller (ed.), *The Letters and Writings of George Frideric Handel* (Dresden, 1935), p. 40.

2 Ibid.

3 Ibid., p. 41.

4 Ibid., p. 42.

5 Quoted in Luckett, *Handel's* Messiah, p. 118.

6 *Memoirs of Dr Charles Burney 1726–69* (University of Nebraska Press, 1988), p. 39.

7 For example, David Hunter, in *The Lives of George Frideric Handel* (Woodbridge, 2016), p. 363.

8 Laurence Whyte, *Original Poems on Various Subjects* (Dublin, 1742).

9 *Faulkner's Dublin Journal*, 27 March 1742.

10 Ibid., 10 April 1742.

11 *Dublin News-Letter*, 14 April 1742.

12 *Faulkner's Dublin Journal*, 14 April 1742.

13 Ibid., 14 April 1742.

14 Thomas Davis, *Memoirs of David Garrick* (1780), p. 54.

15 Donald Burrows, *Handel:* Messiah, p. 20.

CHAPTER 5 THE MYSTERIOUS MR JENNENS

1 Handel to Jennens, 29 December 1741; Muller (ed.), *Letters and Writings*, p. 42.

2 Jennens to Edward Holdsworth, 5 December 1743, quoted in Ruth Smith, *Charles Jennens: The Man Behind Handel's* Messiah (London, 2012), p. 3.

3 The Reverend George Kelly, quoted in Smith, *Jennens*, p. 21.

4 Jennens to Holdsworth, 17 January 1743, quoted in Smith, *Jennens*, p. 44.

5 Ibid., p. 42.

6 Smith, *Charles Jennens*, p. 41.

7 Jennens to Holdsworth, 10 July 1741, quoted in Keates, *Handel*, p. 282.

8 Ibid.

CHAPTER 6 THE LORD GAVE THE WORD

1 Charles Burney, *An Account of the Musical Performances*, p. 34.

2 Anonymous, quoted in Keates, *Handel*, p. 3.

3 Smith, *Charles Jennens*, p. 53.

4 Newburgh Hamilton, preface to *Samson*, 1743.

5 Ruth Smith, 'Messiah' article in Landgraf and Vickers, *Cambridge Handel Encyclopedia*, p. 417.

CHAPTER 7 COMPOSING MESSIAH

1 Joseph Addison, *The Spectator*, number 405.
2 Quoted by W. S. Rockstro, *The Life of George Frederick Handel* (Cambridge University Press reprint, 2013), p. 239.
3 Larsen, *Handel's* Messiah, p. 15.
4 H. R. Haweis: *Music and Morals* (1873), p. 207.
5 Quoted in Christopher Hogwood, *Handel*, 2nd edn (London, 2007), p. 170.
6 Luckett, *Handel's* Messiah, p. 100.

CHAPTER 8 A WORK IN PROGRESS

1 Charles Burney, *An Account of the Musical Performances*, p. 27.
2 Thomas Sheridan, *Sources of the Disorders of Great Britain* (1756), p. 417.
3 Horace Walpole to Sir Horace Mann, 24 February 1743.
4 Quoted in Smith, *Jennens*, p. 53.
5 *Handel: Letters & Writings*, p. 52.
6 Winton Dean, *Handel's Dramatic Oratorios and Masques* (Cambridge, 1959), p. 456.
7 *The European Magazine*, vol. 47 (1805), p. 85.
8 Quoted in Luckett, *Handel's* Messiah, p. 164.
9 Ibid., p. 167.

CHAPTER 9 FINDING AN AUDIENCE

1 *Universal Spectator*, 19 March 1743.

2 Jennens to Holdsworth, March 1743, quoted in Keates, *Handel*, p. 143.
3 Ibid., p. 139.
4 Ibid., p. 151.
5 Ibid., p. 295.
6 Smith, *Charles Jennens*, p. 56.
7 Anonymous, 1745.
8 Poem published in *Faulkner's Dublin Journal*, 22 December 1744.
9 Keates, *Handel*, p. 351.
10 Sir John Hawkins, *A General History of the Science and Practice of Music*, vol. 5 (London, 1776), p. 359.

CHAPTER 10 BLESSING & HONOUR & GLORY & POWER

1 Anna Seward, quoted in Keates, *Handel*, p. 361.
2 Luckett, *Handel's* Messiah, p. 190.
3 Ibid., p. 198.
4 Charles Cudworth, *Mythistoria Handeliana* [part of a Festschrift for Jens Peter Larsen], (Copenhagen, 1972).
5 Letter of James Beattie, 25 May 1780, in William Forbes, *An Account of the Life and Writings of James Beattie* (1806).
6 *Musical Times*, July 1862.
7 *Musical Times*, July 1880.
8 Ralph Waldo Emerson, Journal, 25 December 1843.
9 *Pall Mall Gazette*, May 1884.
10 George Bernard Shaw, *Music in London*, vol. 2 (London, 1932), p. 65.

11 Donald Burrows, *Handel:* Messiah (Cambridge Music Handbooks Series, 1991), p. 52–3.

12 Thomas Beecham, liner notes to 1959 recording of *Messiah* remastered for CD, issued in 1992 by RCA Victor Gold Seal.

13 Quoted in Luckett, op.cit., p. 240.

14 Edward Fitzgerald, letter to George Crabbe, 4 October 1863, in 'Letters Of Edward Fitzgerald', vol. 2, 1851–66 (Princeton University Press, 2014), p. 497.

BIBLIOGRAPHY

Burrows, Donald, *Handel:* Messiah, Cambridge (Cambridge Music Handbooks Series), 1991

———. *Handel*, Oxford (Oxford Master Musicians Series), 1994

Burrows, Donald (ed.), *The Cambridge Companion to Handel*, Cambridge, 1997

Dean, Winton, *Handel's Dramatic Oratorios and Masques*, Cambridge, 1959

Hogg, Katharine, *Handel the Philanthropist*, London, 2009

Hogwood, Christopher, *Handel*, 2nd edn, London, 2007

Hunter, David, *The Lives of George Frideric Handel*, Woodbridge, 2016

Keates, Jonathan, *Handel: The Man and His Music*, 2nd edn, London, 2008

Landgraf, Annette, and David Vickers, *The Cambridge Handel Encyclopedia*, Cambridge, 2009

Larsen, Jens Peter, *Handel's* Messiah*: Origins, Composition, Sources*, 2nd edn, New York, 1972

Luckett, Richard, *Handel's* Messiah*: A Celebration*, London, 1992

Muller, Eric H. (ed.), *The Letters and Writings of George Frideric Handel*, Dresden, 1935

Myers, Robert Manson, *Handel's* Messiah*: A Touchstone of Taste*, New York, 1948

Shaw, Watkins, *A Textual and Historical Companion to Handel's* Messiah, London, 1965

Smith, Ruth, *Charles Jennens: The Man Behind Handel's* Messiah, London, 2012

INDEX

Credit: Jerry Bauer

Jonathan Keates is a distinguished and prize-winning biographer, novelist and travel writer. The author of *Handel* and *Purcell*, he is chairman of the Venice in Peril fund, a fellow of the Royal Society of Literature and a regular contributor to the *Times Literary Supplement*. He lives in the United Kingdom.